The publisher gratefully acknowledges the generous contribution to this book provided by the Humanities Endowment Fund of the University of California Press Foundation.

Also by Robert Creeley

The Collected Poems of Robert Creeley, 1975–2005

The Collected Poems of
Robert Creeley
1975–2005

UNIVERSITY OF CALIFORNIA PRESS
BERKELEY LOS ANGELES LONDON

University of California Press, one of the most distinguished university presses in the United States, enriches lives around the world by advancing scholarship in the humanities, social sciences, and natural sciences. Its activities are supported by the UC Press Foundation and by philanthropic contributions from individuals and institutions. For more information, visit www.ucpress.edu.

University of California Press
Berkeley and Los Angeles, California

University of California Press, Ltd.
London, England

For acknowledgment of the preface, the epigraphs, and of poems previously published, please see credits, page 639.

Library of Congress Cataloging-in-Publication Data

Creeley, Robert, 1926–
  [Poems]
  The collected poems of Robert Creeley.
    p. cm.
  Includes index.
  Contents: [1] 1945–1975–[2] 1975–2005.
  ISBN-10 0-520-24158-4 (v. 1 : pbk. : alk. paper)
  ISBN-13 978-0-520-24158-9 (v. 1 : pbk. : alk. paper)
  ISBN-10 0-520-24159-2 (v. 2 : alk. paper)
  ISBN-13 978-0-520-24159-6 (v. 2 : alk. paper)
    I. Title.

PS3505.R43A17   2006
811'.54–dc22   2006040498

Manufactured in the United States of America

15   14   13   12   11   10   09   08   07   06
10   9   8   7   6   5   4   3   2   1

This book is printed on New Leaf EcoBook 50, a 100% recycled fiber of which 50% is de-inked post-consumer waste, processed chlorine-free. EcoBook 50 is acid-free and meets the minimum requirements of ANSI/ASTM D 5634-01 (Permanence of Paper).

Contents

Note

AT SEVENTY-FIVE YEARS OLD Robert was as excited by the prospect of the University of California Press's bringing out his *Collected Poems* as he was by the prospect of our moving to Providence, Rhode Island, from Buffalo.

In the hospital in March 2005—on the last night of his life, as it turned out—he asked for the hard drive of his computer, so that he could work the next day on the manuscript for this volume of poetry.

Now I can only guess what he might have done. We had talked about his writing a new preface. He had thought about what he wanted to say: These are my poems. I love them and stand by them.

In retrospect, I realize the courage such an act takes, the courage artists have every day to produce something out of the raw feelings and intimate perceptions of life, then to hold it up to public scrutiny. In reading these poems again, I hear Robert's voice, and I see the last twenty-seven years of my own life laid out, almost a diary. I think of the way I first saw this writing, just words on a page, a little distillation of a day, tender and vulnerable and fresh, a moment, untried, yet a whole world of thought, life, and history in each. Those words, "This is my life's work. I love it and stand by it," are such an affirmation. To come to that moment, to say so clearly, without hesitation. To have that heart. Yes. Here it is. That heart.

If there are poems left out, acknowledgments not made, inadequacies of text or explication, the fault is mine. I plead inexperience. But I know this work stands on its own.

Onward.

PENELOPE CREELEY
PROVIDENCE, NOVEMBER 19, 2005

Preface: Old Poetry

Ay, tear her tattered ensign down!
Long has it waved on high,
And many an eye has danced to see
That banner in the sky;
Beneath it rung the battle shout,
And burst the cannon's roar; —
The meteor of the ocean air
Shall sweep the clouds no more.
—OLIVER WENDELL HOLMES

Even to speak becomes an unanticipated drama, because where one has come to, and where it is one now has to go, have no language any longer specific. We all will talk like that, yet no one will understand us.

When I was a young man, I felt often as if I were battling for the integrity of my habits of speech, my words, my friends, my life. W. C. Williams had put it most clearly, and with the expected emphasis of that time: "When a man makes a poem, makes it, mind you, he takes words as he finds them interrelated about him and composes them—without distortion which would mar their exact significances—into an intense expression of his perceptions and ardors that they may constitute a revelation in the speech that he uses." In the furies, then, of the war and the chaos of a disintegrating society, I felt a place, of useful honor and possibility, in those words.

As though one might dignify, make sufficient, all the bits and pieces one had been given, all the remnants of a family, the confusions of name and person, flotsam, even the successes quickly subsumed by the next arrival.

This was originally published as the preface to *So There: Poems 1976–1983* (New York: New Directions, 1998). On July 1, 1998, Robert Creeley wrote to Peggy Fox of New Directions about his use of italics in this preface: "The paragraphs in italics are simply to have a variation of 'voice,' the italicized sections being more reflective, reacting to the subject or thought in mind, the non-italicized sections being the forward statement, so to speak. Otherwise quotations are in quotes."

And after that, the next—and then the next again. How would one ever catch up?

There was no identity, call it, for the poet in my world. It was only in my mind and imagination that any of it was real. "Only the imagination is real," Williams said. It felt particularly American to have no viable tradition, no consequence of others seemingly sufficient, my elders contested if not dismissed. Yet, paradoxically, we were exceptionally chauvinistic, felt finally a contempt for the poetry of that old world, the European, which nonetheless still intimidated us. All the arts, it seemed, fought to become dominant in whatever scale they might be weighed in—Abstract Expressionists vs. the School of Paris, John Cage vs. Benjamin Britten, Louis Zukofsky vs. W. H. Auden. Already that person as *myself* had become an insistent *we*, a plural of swelling confidence.

They say you can be sure of three things in America, in any company, and you can always let them be known without fear of social reprisal. One, that you know nothing about opera. Two, that you know nothing about poetry. Three, that you speak no language other than English. Is that true?

René Thom somewhere speaks of poetry's being like humor. It stays local because it uses its means with such particularity. Just so, a friend tells me of a friend of his, a fellow student who is Japanese, saying, "What the Americans think is interesting in Japanese poetry misses the point entirely. They miss the essence, the kernel, the substance of its effects." Another friend once told me he had written a haiku whose second line was a measured one mile long.

"A Nation of nothing but poetry . . ." Who owns it? "He is the president of regulation . . ." How did that go? How is it (ever) far if you think it? Where are we? It was poetry that got us here, and now we have to go too. "I'll hate to leave this earthly paradise . . ." Is there a country? "Image Nation . . ."

Despairs since I was a little boy seem always the same. No money, not enough to eat, no clothes, sick, forced out. No job or identity. Years ago, driving back to San Geronimo Miramar from Guatemala City in the early evening, I caught sight of a body lying out into the narrow road, so stopped to see what had happened. It was a man, drunk, trying to kill himself in that bleak way. He had spent all his life's accumulated money in one day's drinking, and had lost his identity card as well—and so he no longer actually existed, in any record. I kept trying, uselessly, persistently, to help.

We will keep ourselves busy enough, working with our various procedures and values. There'll be no irony or blame. Whoever we imagine it's for will either hear us out, else leave with a sense of better things to do. Better we learn a common song?

Seventy-two my next birthday and still feeling good, still pouring it out. Hardly a day goes by that I don't think of something, either to do or to be done. Stay *busy* seems to be it. But most it's like coming back again to childhood, dumbly, even uselessly. When I saw my old school chums at our fiftieth reunion, I realized I hadn't seen them—Fred, Marion, Katie, Ralph and Patsy—since we were fourteen. Now we were over sixty, all the work done but for whatever was left to tidy up. It was a great, unexpected relief not to have to say what we had earned, merited, lost or coveted. It was all done.

So now for the bridge, as in music, carries one over—

Trust to good verses then;
They only will aspire,
When pyramids, as men,
Are lost i' th' funeral fire.

And when all bodies meet,
In Lethe to be drowned,
Then only numbers sweet
With endless life are crown'd.

—ROBERT HERRICK

With love, for Herrick and Zukofsky.

BUFFALO, N.Y.
FEB. 8, 1998

Author's Note

Insofar as the specific lines of these various poems are, in each case, the defining rhythmic unit, it is crucial that their integrity be recognized, else a false presumption of a poem's underlying beat may well occur in those cases where a runover line, i.e., a line broken by the limits of a page's dimensions, may be mistaken for the author's intent. Therefore all such lines are preceded by this symbol (◁)* and are indented the characteristic space (1 em) from the poem's left margin. Read them as if they were one with the lines which they follow.

R.C.

*This note appeared in *The Collected Poems of Robert Creeley, 1945–1975*. Please note that in this second volume of collected poems, however, a slightly different symbol (◁) has been used to identify runover lines.

The Collected Poems of Robert Creeley, 1975-2005

Hello: A Journal, February 29–May 3, 1976

Wellington, New Zealand

"That's the way
(that's the way

I like it
(I like it"

.

Clouds coming close.

.

Never forget
clouds dawn's
pink red acid
gash—!

.

Here comes
one now!

.

Step out into
space. Good
morning.

.

Well, sleep,
man.

.

Not *man,*
mum's
the word.

.

What do you
think those hills
are going to do now?

·

They got
all the
lights on −
all the people.

·

You know
if you never
you won't

                    2/29

It's the scale
that's attractive,
and the water
that's around it.

·

Did the young
couple come
only home
from London?

Where's the world
one wants.

·

Singular,
singular,

one
by one.

·

I wish I
could see the stars.

.

Trees *want*
to be still?
Winds
won't let them?

.

Anyhow,
it's night now.

Same clock ticks
in these different places.

3/1

Dunedin

River wandering down
below in the widening green
fields between the hills—
and the sea and the town.

Time settled, or waiting,
or about to be. People,
the old couple, the two babies,
beside me—the so-called

aeroplane. Now
be born,
be born.

.

I'll never
see you,
want you,
have you,
know you —

I'll never.

·

"Somebody's got to pay
for the squeaks in the bed."

·

Such quiet,
dog's scratch at door —

pay for it all?

·

Walking
and talking.

Thinking
and drinking.

·

Night.
Light's out.

3/3

"*Summa wancha*

out back"

Australia

.

"Sonny Terry,
"Brownie McGhee"

in Dunedin (in
Dunedin

3/4

10:30 AM: Ralph Hotere's

Warm.
See sun shine.
Look across valley at houses.
Chickens squawk.
Bright glint off roofs.
Water's also,
in bay, in distance.
Hills.

3/5

Christchurch

You didn't think you
could do it but you did.

You didn't do it
but you did.

.

Catching Cold

I want to lay down
and die—
someday—but
not now.

.

South, north, east, west,
man—home's best.

.

Nary an exit
in Christchurch.

Only
wee holes.

3/9

Out Window: Taylor's Mistake

Silver,
lifting
light—

mist's
faintness.

.

Friend Says of Job

FOR BARRY SOUTHAM

You get to see all kinds of life
like man chasing wife
in the driveway
with their car.

Mutual property!
They want to sell their house?

.

Elsewise absences,
eyes a grey blue,
tawny Austrian

hair—the voice,
speaking, *there.*

.

Hermione, in the garden,
"weeping at grief?"

Stone-statued single woman—
eyes alive.

.

Milton über Alles

When I consider
how my life is spent
ere half my years
on this vast blast

are o'er . . .

.

Reasoned recognitions—
feelings fine.

.

Welcome
to the world,
it's still
pretty much the same.

That kiwi
on yon roof
is a symbol,
but the ocean

don't change.
It's all *round!*
Don't
let them kid you.

3/11

Palmerston North

Soup

I know what you'd say
if I could ask you—
but I'm tired of it—
no word, nothing again.

Letter from guy says,
"she looks well,
happy, working hard—"
Forget it.

I'm not there.
I'm really here,
sitting,
with my hat on.

It's a great day
in New Zealand
more or less.
I'm not alone in this.

Lady out window hangs clothes,
reds and blues—
basket, small kid,
clothespins in mouth.

Do I want to fuck,
or eat?
No problem.
There's a telephone.

I know what you mean,
now "down under" here,
that each life's
got its own condition

to find,
to get on with.
I suppose it's
letting go, finally,

that spooks me.
And of course my arms
are full as usual.
I'm the only one I know.

May I let this be
West Acton, and
myself six? No,
I don't travel that way

despite memories,
all the dear or awful
passages apparently
I've gone through.

Back to the weather,
and dripping nose
I truly wanted to forget here,
but haven't—

ok, old buddy,
no projections, no regrets.
You've been a dear friend
to me in my time.

If it's New Zealand
where it ends,
that makes a weird sense
too. I'd never have guessed it.

Say that all the ways
are one — *consumatum est* —
like some soup
I'd love to eat with you.

3/16

This wide, shallow bowl,
the sun, earth here
moving easy, slow
in the fall, the air
with its lightness, the
underchill now — flat, far out,
to the mountains and the forest.
Come home to its song?

.

Sitting at table —
good talk
with good people.

.

River's glint, wandering
path of it.

Old trees grown tall,
maintain,
look down on it all.

.

Bye-bye, kid says,
girl, about five —
peering look,
digs my one eye.

·

Sun again, on table,
smoke shaft of cigarette,
ticking watch,
chirr of cicadas —
all world, all mind, all heart.

3/17

Wellington

Here again,
shifting days,

on the street.
The people of my life

faded,
last night's dreams,

echoes now.
The vivid sky, blue,

sitting here in the sun —
could I let it go?

Useless question?
Getting old?

.

I want to be a dog,
when I die—

a dog, a dog.

.

Bruce & Linley's House

Fire back of grate
in charming stove
sits in the chimney hole,
cherry red—
but orange too.

.

Mrs. Manhire saw me
on plane to Dunedin,
but was too shy to speak
in her lovely Scots accent.

We meet later,
and she notes the sounds are
not very sweet
in sad old Glasgow.

But my wee toughness,
likewise particularity,
nonetheless come
by blood from that city.

.

Love

Will you be dust,
reading this?

Will you be sad
when I'm gone.

3/19

Sit Down

Behind things
or in front of them,
always a goddamn
adamant number stands

up and shouts,
I'm here, I'm here!
—Sit down.

·

Mother and son
get up,
sit down.

·

Night

Born and bred
in Wellington
she said—

Light high,
street black,
singing still,

"Born & bred
in Wellington,
she said—"

.

Doggie Bags

Don't take
the steak
I ain't
Dunedin

.

The dishes
to the sink
if you've
Dunedin

.

Nowhere
else to go
no I'm not
Dunedin

    .

Ever if
again home
no roam
(at the inn)

Dunedin

    .

Maybe

Maybe
this way again

someday —
thinking, last night,

of Tim Hardin, girl singing,
"Let me be your rainy day man . . ."

What's the time, dear.
What's happening.

    .

Stay

in Dunedin

for

forever

and a day.

      ·

Thinking light,
whitish blue,
sun's
shadow on
the porch
floor.

     ·

Why, in Wellington,
all the "Dunedin"—

Why here
there.

         3/21

Hamilton

Hamilton Hotel

Magnolia tree out window
here in Hamilton—
years and years ago
the house, in France,

called *Pavillion des Magnolias*,
where we lived and Charlotte
was born, and time's gone
so fast—.

.

Singing undersounds,
birds, cicadas—
overcast grey day.

Lady far off across river,
sitting on bench there,
crossed legs, alone.

.

If the world's one's
own experience of it,

then why walk around
in it, or think of it.

More would be more
than one could know

alone, more than myself's
small senses, of it.

3/22

Auckland

So There

FOR PENELOPE

Da. Da. Da da.
Where is the song.
What's wrong
with life

ever. More?
Or less—
days, nights,
these

days. *What's gone*
is gone forever
every time, old friend's
voice here. I want

to stay, somehow,
if I could—
if I would? Where else
to go.

The sea here's out
the window, old
switcher's house, vertical,
railroad blues, *lonesome*

whistle, etc. Can you
think of Yee's Cafe
in Needles, California
opposite the train

station—can you keep
it ever
together, old buddy, talking
to yourself again?

Meantime some *yuk*
in Hamilton has blown
the whistle on a charming
evening I wanted

to remember otherwise—
the river there, that
afternoon, sitting,
friends, wine & chicken,

watching the world go by.
Happiness, happiness—
so simple. What's
that anger is that

competition—sad!—
when this at least
is free,
to put it mildly.

My aunt Bernice
in Nokomis,
Florida's last act,
a poem for Geo. Washington's

birthday. Do you want
to say "it's bad"?
In America, old sport,
we shoot first, talk later,

or just take you out to dinner.
No worries, or not
at the moment,
sitting here eating bread,

cheese, butter, white wine —
like Bolinas, "Whale Town,"
my home, like they say,
in America. It's *one* world,

it can't be another.
So the beauty,
beside me, rises,
looks now out window —

and breath keeps on breathing,
heart's pulled in
a sudden deep, sad
longing, to want

to stay — be another
person some day,
when I grow up.
The world's somehow

forever that way
and its lovely, roily,
shifting shores, sounding now,
in my ears. My ears?

Well, what's on my head
as two skin appendages,
comes with the package.
I don't want to

argue the point.
Tomorrow
it changes, gone,
abstract, new places—

moving on. Is this
some old-time weird
Odysseus trip
sans paddle—up

the endless creek?
Thinking of you,
baby, thinking
of all the things

I'd like to say and do.
Old-fashioned time
it takes to be
anywhere, at all.

Moving on. Mr. Ocean,
Mr. Sky's
got the biggest blue eyes
in creation—

here comes the sun!
While we can,
let's do it, let's
have fun.

            3/26

Sidney, Australia

Now

Hard to believe
it's all *me*

whatever
this world

of space & time,
this place,

body,
white,

inutile,
fumbling at the mirror.

                     3/27

Yah

 Sure I fell in love —
"with a very lovely person."
 You'd love her too.
"She's lovely."

         .

Funny what your head
does, waking up

in room, world,
you never saw before,

each night new.
Beautiful view, like they say,

this time, Sydney—
who's always been a friend of mine.

Boats out there, dig it?
Trees so green you could

eat them, grass too.
People, by god—

"so you finally got here?"
Yeah, passing through.

.

One person
and a dog.

.

Woman staggering
center of street—

wop!
Messy.

All in
the mind.

.

Long
legged
dark
man

I think.

.

Hey Cheryl!
Talk

to me.
Yiss?

Say it like this.

    .

I love
Australia —

it's so big
and fuzzy

in bed.

    .

Then

Don't go
to the mountains,

again — not
away, mad. Let's

talk it out, you
never went anywhere.

I did — and here
in the world, looking back

on so-called life
with its impeccable

talk and legs and breasts,
I loved you

but not as some
gross habit, please.

Your voice
so quiet now,

so vacant, for me,
no sound, on the phone,

no clothes, on the floor,
no face, no hands,

—if I didn't want
to be here, I wouldn't

be here, and would
be elsewhere? Then.

3/28

Window

Aching sense
of being

person—body in-
side, out—

the houses, sky,
the colors, sounds.

3/29

Places

All but
for me and Paul.

    •

Off
of.

       3/30

En Route Perth

For Cheryl

Sitting here in limbo, "there are
sixteen different shades of red."

Sitting here in limbo, there are
people walking through my head.

If I thought I'd think it different,
I'd just be dumber than I said.

    •

Hearing sounds in
plane's landing gear lowering:

I don' wanna

    3/31

Singapore

Men

Here, on the wall
of this hotel in
Singapore, there's a

picture, of a woman,
big-breasted, walking,
blue-coated, with

smaller person — both
followed by a house men
are carrying. It's a day

in the life of the world.
It tells you, somehow,
what you ought to know.

·

Getting fainter, in the world,
fearing something's fading,
deadened, tentative responses —
go hours without eating,
scared without someone to be
with me. These empty days.

·

Growth, trees, out window's
reminiscent of other days,

other places, years ago,
a kid in Burma, war,

fascinated, in jungle,
happily not shot at,

hauling the dead and dying
along those impossible roads

to nothing much could help.
Dreaming, of home, the girl

left behind, getting drunk,
getting laid, getting beaten

out of whorehouse one night.
So where am I now.

.

Patience gets
you the next place.

So they say.

.

Some huge clock
somewhere said it was
something like sixteen

or twenty hours later
or earlier there, going
around and around.

.

Blue Rabbit

Things going quiet
got other things

in mind. That rabbit's
scared of me! I can't

drag it out by the ears
again just to look.

.

I'll remember the dog,
with the varicolored,

painted head, sat
beside me, in Perth,

while I was talking
to the people

in the classroom —
and seemed to listen.

4/4

Manila, the Philippines

Country Western

Faint dusky light
at sunset – park,

Manila – people
flooding the flatness,
speakers, music:

"Yet I did

"the best I could

"with what I had . . ."

.

Here Again

No sadness
in the many –
only the one,
separate, looks
to see another
come. So it's
all by myself
again, one
way or another.

.

Later

Later than any time
can tell me, finding
ways now as I can—

any blame, anything
I shouldn't do, any
thing forgotten, any way

to continue, this little
way, these smaller ways—
pride I had, what I thought

I could do, had done.
Anyone, anything, still
out there—is there some

one possible, something
not in mind still as
my mind, my way. I

persist only in wanting,
only in thinking, only now
in waiting, for that way

to be the way I can
still let go, still want, and
still let go, and want to.

4/5

Manila

Life goes on living,
sitting in chair here

in café at Domestic Airport—
heat stirring my skin & bones,

and people like dusty
old movie, Peter Lorre, and

I don't see no criminals
looking at nobody, only

myriad people on this final
island of the ultimate world.

    ·

Each time *sick loss*
feeling starts to hit me,
think of *more* than that,
more than "I" thought of.

    ·

Early morning still—
"announcing the ah-ri-

val" of world in little,
soft, wet, sticky pieces.

    ·

You can tilt the world
by looking at it sideways—

or you can put it up-
side down by standing on

your head—and underneath,
or on end, or this way,

or that, the waves come in,
and grass grows.

·

Breaking Up Is Hard to Do

"Don't take your love
"away from me—

"Don't leave my heart
"in misery . . ."

I know that it's
true. I know.

·

One day here
seems like years now

since plane came in
from Singapore—

heart in a bucket,
head in hand.

·

Falling to sleep nights
like losing balance—

crash!—wake to bright
sunlight, time to go!

Cebu

Cebu

Magellan was x'ed here
but not much now left,

seemingly, of that event
but for hotel's name —

and fact of boats filling
the channel. And the churches,

of course, as Mexico, as all of
Central and South America.

Driving in from the airport,
hot, trying to get bearings —

witness easy seeming pace of the place,
banana trees, mangos, the high

vine grapes on their trellises.
But particularly the people moseying

along. Also the detention home
for boys, and another casual prison

beside the old airport now
used for light planes. I saw

in a recent paper a picture
of a triangular highrise in Chicago,

downtown, a new prison there,
looking like a modern hotel.

Also in Singapore there are
many, many new buildings—

crash housing for the poor,
that hurtles them skyward off

the only physical thing they
had left. Wild to see clotheslines,

flapping shirts, pants, dresses,
something like thirty stories up!

I'd choose, no doubt dumbly,
to keep my feet on the ground—

and I like these houses here,
open-sided, thatched roofed—

that could all be gone in a flash,
or molder more slowly

back into humus. One doesn't
finally want it all forever,

not stopped there, in abstract
time. Whatever, it's got to

be yielded, let go of, it can't
live any longer than it has to.

Being human, at times I
get scared, of dying, growing

old, and think my body's
possibly the exception to all

that I know has to happen.
It isn't, and some of those

bananas are already rotten,
and no doubt there are vacant

falling-down houses, and boats
with holes in their bottoms

no one any longer cares about.
That's all right, and I can

dig it, yield to it, let what
world I do have be the world.

In this room the air-conditioner
echoes the southwest of America—

my mother-in-law's, in Albuquerque,
and I wonder what she's doing

today, and if she's happy there,
as I am here, with these green

walls, and the lights on, and
finally loving everything I know.

4/7

Morning

Dam's broke,
head's a
waterfall.

Davao

Davao Insular Hotel

You couldn't get it
off here in a million

obvious years, shrubs cut
to make animals, bluish,

reddish, purple lights
illuminating the pool—

and the only lady within
miles to talk to tells me

she got culture-shocked by
multiple single-seat tv sets

in bus stations, airports, in
the States. So we're single

persons, so the jungle's
shrunk to woods, and

people are Jim and Mary—
have a drink. I can't

believe the solution's this
place either, three hundred

calculated persons to each
and every family unit,

sucking like mad to get fed.
Extended, distended—no

intent ever to be more or
less than the one sits next

to you, holds your hand,
and, on occasion, fucks.

4/8

Baler

Apocalypse Now

Waiting to see if
Manila's a possi-
bility, yellow plane
of Francis F. Coppola
on tarmac fifty
yards away—kids,
coins, flipping, air
wet, rather warm—
no movies today,
friends—just sit
in air, on bench, be-
fore cantina, listen
to words of mouths
talking Tagalog,
and "I swear I
love my husband"—

I could spend quite
a bit of time here,
but by nine in
the morning, I hope
I can get home.

.

Wrong: white man's
over-reach, teeth
eating tongue, spoken
beforehand, al-
ready.

4/10

Singapore

Evening

Walking street back here,
the main drag for the money,
and lights just going on,
day faded, people hot, distracted—

one person, walking, feeling older
now, heavier, from chest to hips
a lump won't move with my legs,
and all of it tireder, slower—

flashes in store windows, person
with somewhat silly hat on,
heavy-waisted, *big,* in the company,
and out of step, out of place—

back to the lone hotel room,
sit here now, writing this,
thinking of the next step,
and when and how to take it.

.

Split mind, hearing voice—
two worlds, two places.

4/11

Talking

Faded back last night
into older dreams, some

boyhood lost innocences.
The streets have become inaccessible

and when I think of people,
I am somehow not one of them.

Talking to the doctor-
novelist, he read me a poem

of a man's horror, in Vietnam,
child and wife lost to him—

his own son sat across from me,
about eight, thin, intent—

and myself was like a huge,
fading balloon, that could hear

but not be heard, though we
talked and became clear friends.

I wanted to tell him I was
an honest, caring man. I wanted

the world to be more simple,
for all of us. His wife said,

driving back, that my hotel's bar
was a swinging place in the '50s.

It was a dark, fading night.
She spoke quickly, obliquely,

along for the ride, sitting
in the front seat beside him.

I could have disappeared, gone
away, seen them fading too,

war and peace, death,
life, still no one.

.

Why want
to be so *one*
when it's not
enough?

.

Down and
down, over
and out.

                    4/13

Kuala Lumpur, Malaysia

Old Saying

There is no
more.

    •

Start again
from the beginning then.

4/14

Hotel Lobby

Sun out window's
a blessing, air's
warmth and wetness.

The people fade,
melt, in the mind.

    •

No scale, no congruence,
enough.

    •

This must be some
time-stream, persons
all the same.

    •

How call back,
or speak forward?

Keep the physical
literal.

    •

Play on it,
jump up.

    •

I don't
look like
anybody
here!

    •

Funny how
people pick
their noses.

Riding with Sal

FOR SALLEH

Pounding VW motor
past the people, cars —

hot day in downtown
Kuala Lumpur, and the

Chinese-lunch-style
conversation's still in mind,

"do Americans look *down*
on Asians?" Is the world

round, or flat, is it
one, or two, or many—

and what's a Muslim
like you doing here

anyhow. Breeze lifts,
sun brightens at edges,

trees crouch under
towering hotel's walls.

Go to Afghanistan and
be Sufis together, brother,

dance to *that* old in-
veterate wisdom after all.

.

Sufi Sam Christian

Lift me into heaven
slowly 'cause my back's

sore and my mind's too
thoughtful, and I'm not

even sure I want to go.

.

Lunch and After

I don't want to leave
so quickly, the lovely

faces, surrounding, human
terms so attractive. And

the world, the *world,* we
could think of, *here,* to-

gether, a flash of instant, a
million years of time.

Don't, myself, be an
old man yet, I want to

move out and into this
physical, endless place.

Sun's dazzling shine now
back of the towering clouds,

and sounds of builders'
pounding, faint, distant

buzz of traffic. Mirror's
in front of me, hat's on

head, under it, human
face, my face, reddened,

it seems, lined, grey's
in beard and mustache—

not only *myself* but an-
other man has got to

at last walk out and into
another existence, out there,

that haze that softens those trees,
all those other days to come.

     .

War & Peace

Cannot want not to
want, cannot. Thinks

later, acts
now.

     .

Hotel Merlin

On the seventeenth
floor of this

modern building, in
room I accepted

gratefully, bed I
lay down on—

vow to think
more responsibly?

Vow to be
kinder to

mother (dead), brothers
(dead), sister—

who loves me?
Will I now see

this world as
possible arrangement.

Will I eat
less, work more

for common ends?
Will I turn from friends,

who are not friends?
Will judgment,

measure
of such order,

rule me?
Or will flash of willful

impulse
still demand

whatever life,
whatever death.

.

Seventeenth Floor: Echoes of Singapore

No one's going to
see me naked up here.

My only chance is
to jump.

4/15

Up Here

Place in mind
or literal, out window,
"too abstract"—

a long way down
to the street—
or home.

·

Time

Can't live,
mindless,
in present—

can't make past,
or future,
enough place.

4/16

Hong Kong

Remember

Sweltering, close
dreams of a
possible heaven —

before sleeping mind,
before waking
up to dead day.

.

Hong Kong Window

Seemingly awash
in this
place, *here* —

egocentric
abstraction —
no one

else but
me again,
and people,

people as if
behind glass,
close

but untouchable.
What
was the world

I'd thought of,
who
was to be there?

The buildings
lean in
this window,

hotel's abstraction,
cars
like toys pass,

below,
fourteen stories
down

on those streets.
In park
kids wade

in a pool.
Grey day,
in spring,

waits for rain.
"What's
the question?"

Who asks it,
which *me*
of what life.

                .

Park

Like in the Brownie Books—
people below, in distance,
like little moving dots of color,
look at 'em go!

   ·

Buildings against hillsides
waiting for night
to make a move.

   ·

Something about the vertical
and the horizontal
out of whack possibly,

viz., the buildings
look like they could walk,
and in the flat park,

below, the people are
walking, and running even,
but I can't put the two together.

   ·

Sign

"SIEMENS" not
semen's, and I don't
see men's—and I don't
know what it means.

   ·

Buildings

Why not make them
higher, and higher, and
higher—until they fall down?

.

Something about raw side
of cut cliff, with building
jammed against it, still hurts.

.

With world now
four billion, you
haven't even started yet.

.

Sentimental
about earth
and water,

and people?
Still got enough
to share?

.

But if you don't,
you won't
have it long.

.

The money's singing
in the walls of this building.

    ·

Sun's out. Big
lazy clouds float
over the buildings.
Thank god.

    ·

Park

Why did that man
fly the kid's kite
precisely into the trees

when a wide space
of bare ground was
a few feet away. Was it

the women, with them,
sitting on the park bench,
didn't want to move.

    ·

Kid's face, lifting
big yellow speed boat
with proper gas motor

out of pool after
it's conked out, all
the other kids around,

watching him. He's in
some sad defensive place
now. It's still his.

            •

Lots of older
women here talking
to younger women.

Now one, by herself,
pregnant, walks by.
Her legs look thin from the back.

            •

This park is really used.
It's got bare ground
like in Boston.

            •

Can see tennis players,
with roller skaters behind them.
"One world."

            •

Trees dancing now.
They dig it.

            •

And you can't
be alone for long.

            4/19

Hong Kong—Last Words

I want to get off
the fucking world and
sit down in a chair,
and be there.

4/21

Tokyo, Japan

Things to Do in Tokyo

FOR TED BERRIGAN

Wake up.
Go to sleep.
Sit *zazen* five days
in five minutes.

Talk
to the beauty next to me
on plane, go-
ing to San Francisco.

Think it's all a dream.
Return
"passport, wallet and ticket"
to man I'd taken them from.

No mistakes.
This time.
Remember mother
ashed in an instant.

No tears.
No way, other than this one.
Wander. Sing
songs from memory. Tell

classical Chinese poet
Bob Dylan's the same.
Sit again in air.
Be American.

Love. Eat
Unspeakable Chicken—
"old in vain."
Lettuce, tomato—

bread. Be humble.
Think again.
Remy Martin is
Pete Martin's brother?

Drink. Think
of meeting Richard Brautigan,
and brandy, years ago.
(All the wonder,

all the splendor,
of Ezra Pound!)
Don't be dismayed,
don't be cheap.

No Hong Kong,
no nothing.
Be on the way
to the way

to the way.
Every day's happy,
sad. "That's the way"
to think. Love

people, all over.
Begin at the beginning,
find the end.
Remember everything,

forget it. Go on,
and on. Find ecstasy,
forget it.
Eat chicken entirely,

recall absent friends.
Love wife
by yourself, love
women, men,

children.
Drink, eat
"and be merry." Sleep
when you can. Dogs

possibly human? —
not cats or birds.
Let all openings be openings.
Simple holes.

Virtue is people,
mind's eye in trees,
sky above,
below's water, earth.

Keep the beat
Confucian — "who
controls." Think man's
possibly beauty's brother,

or husband.
No matter, no mind.
It's here, it's around.
Sing

deliberately.
Love all relations,
be father to daughters,
sons. Respect

wife's previous residence
in Tokyo, stories
she told. All time,
all mind, all

worlds,
can't exist
by definition —
are one.

.

The Winner

I'm going to beat
everything I can.

.

American Love

A big-assed
beauty!

.

Memory

A fresh
sea breeze.

.

The

[Thinking of L.Z., "That one could, etc."]

A's

4/21

Kyoto

Inn / Kyoto

Suddenly *here*,
let down, into room,
as if bare—

tea,
and packaged small cake,
food also for thought—

squat
on bottom, floor,
feel heavy—

but sure of place,
in place.
Where time's been,

years, a humor
can't
be absent.

So woman, my age,
who's led me
through corridor,

slides door open,
comes into room again,
laughs

at misunderstanding.
"The bath
tonight?" No,

tomorrow
night. "Eat
Japanese

in the morning?"
Eat –
in the morning.

4/23

For Benny

Kids of Kyoto
visible through split
bamboo screen –

across canal
to street. One lifts
her skirt, blue,

to reveal red underpants
her friend
then examines.

It's a small world,
these subtle
wooden houses,

sliding screens,
mats on floor,
water running

so often within hearing –
all that, and the
keeper of this tiny inn,

a woman, laughs,
thank god, as I crash
from wall to wall.

I'm sitting here,
having seen six
temples this morning,

wondering if I lack
religion. Old man
now passes,

shaved head, grey clothes,
and a woman stops
to look in her purse.

It's just about
four o'clock —
it's grey, shifting clouds,

no rain as yet.
I like it, and I'm happy
to sleep on the floor,

which I do, like a log.
It's truly time
to study the water,

passing, each specific
ripple, flicker
of light — take

everything I know
and put it out there,
where it's got to go.

4/24

Later

Drunks leaning on your arm,
and the endless drinking
in Japan, and going
to Osaka—

"where the men chew tobacker
and the women wiggy-
waggy-woo . . ."

.

No way
today.

.

Cheap Thrill

Write in air
with flourishes.

                    4/25

Sapporo

Women

I'll always
look that way
to see
where I'm going.

                    4/27

Seoul, Korea

Seoul Sounds

FOR ENGLISH LITERARY SOCIETY OF KOREA

Weird, flat seeming—
tho' mountains surround—
old Seoul!

And they's got
soul-food
and soul-folk, these

instant Irish.
Syncretic,
someone said, when

I'd asked, was there
Confucian true root?
Much mixed in,

thus, but tough,
hold to it,
push back.

Sentimental,
like Americans—
cry and laugh!

Once in, confusions
grow less,
though day's grey

and I'm stretched,
got to talk
in an hour.

But here
in this room, there's
a peace, and some hope

I can say it,
make words sing
human truth:

If one's still
of *many,*
then one's not alone—

If one lives
with *people,*
then one has a home.

.

Place

FOR MARIA

Let's take
any
of the information of

this world and
make a picture,
dig. The

fact of things,
you know, the
edges, pieces

of so-called
reality, will doubtless
surface. So

surfaces—abstract
initial e-
vent—are—

god knows, god
possibly cares, and
now some *other*

"thing" is
the case, viz., "I
love you," now
I'm here.

4/29

Maria Speaks

Still morning
again. "Mendel's
successor"—the

Zen brother
next door
who kept

insects in
a jar—perfected
listening

to things
"spreading their legs,"
"fish tanks filled with bugs."

.

Kids / Seoul

Watching incredible kids
cross street, against traffic,
pushing a bike—

little girl leads, hand
on the handlebars—
heart's so content

to be pleased,
to find joy,
like they say,

can be simple.

.

Talk

Talking Ginsbergian
chop-talk's
a pleasure—see

person, find face
right over middle.
Look down for shoes,

legs just above.
Something to look at,
and something to love!

4/30

Taegu

There

Miles back
in the wake,
days faded—

nights sleep seemed
falling down
into some deadness—

killing it,
thinking dullness,
thinking body

was dying.
Then
you changed it.

    •

Clock

How to live
with some plan
puts the days

into emptiness,
fills time
with time?

.

Not much
left to go on—
it's moving
out.

.

Gifts

Giving me things,
weights accumulate.

I wish
you wouldn't—

I wish we
could eat

somewhere,
drink.

.

Friend

"Father's dead,"
feel flutter,

wings, trying
to beat the dark.

    .

Going Home

You'll love me
later, after

you've tried
everything else

and got tired.
But body's

catching up,
time's lost

as possibility.
Mind's no longer

a way
tonight.

                    5/1

Seoul

Korean slang
for Americans:

"hellos"

.

9:45 AM

Sitting in plane still
in airport, bright

tight sunlight
thru window, guy

sitting in seat alongside,
Japanese, flips pages

of white book. In the aisle
people wander, looking for seats.

.

Nobody here to love
enough to want to.

.

American chichi traveler
just flashed past, her
long brown hair wide open!

.

Catches pillow
flipped to her—

In charge.

.

Probable Truth

It's best
to die
when you can.

Tokyo

Place

Long gone time —
waves still crash in?
Fall coming on?

.

Shifting head to
make transition, rapid
mind to think it.

.

Halfway to wherever,
places, things
I used to do.

.

Out Here

People having a good time
in the duty-free shop,
Tokyo Airport —

can you knock it. Recall
Irving Layton's classic line
re his mother: "her face

was flushed with bargains, etc."
Can't finally think
the world is good guys

and bad guys, tho' these creeps
drive me back into this
corner of the bar—but I'd

choose it anyhow, sit,
hoping for company. A few
minutes ago I was thinking:

"Fuck me, Ruby, right
between the eyes!"
Not any more, it's later,

and is going to get later yet
'fore I get on plane, go home,
go somewhere else at least.

It's raining, outside, in
this interjurisdictional headquarters.
I'm spooked, tired, and approaching

my fiftieth birthday. Appropriately
I feel happy, and sad,
at the same time. I think of

Peter Warshall's amulet I've worn
round my neck for two months now—
turtle, with blue bead cosmos—

that's enough. Nancy Whitefield's
childhood St. Christopher's medal
has stayed safe in the little box

wherein I keep fingernail clippers,
and a collar button, and several
small stones I picked up on a beach.

People still around but
they're fading out now to
get another plane. Hostess,

picking up her several fried chicken
quick lunches, smiles at me,
going past. Guy with spoonbill

blue cap and apparently
American bicentennial mottoes
on front of it, orders a San Miguel

beer. Now he knocks on glass door,
adjacent, I guess his wife's on
the other side. Days, days

and nights, and more of same—
and who wins, loses, never
that simple to figure out.

I'll be a long way away
when you read this—and I won't
remember what I said.

　　　·

Dear

You're getting fat,
dear.

　　　·

Then

Put yourself where you'll be
in five hours
and look back

and see if you'd do the same
the way you're doing it
all the time.

.

That's not easy
to think about.

.

It was
once.

.

Which Is to Say

You could do everything
you could do.

.

Killing time
by not looking
by killing time.

.

Jaws

See one more person
chewing something
I'll eat them both.

.

Kid's giggling
obbligato.

.

No one's going
anywhere.

.

Epic

Save some room
for my epic.

.

Absence makes
a hole.

.

Any story
begins somewhere

and any other story
begins somewhere else.

.

Here

Since I can't
kill anyone,
I'd better
sit still.

    .

She's Back!

Styles of drinking, the cool
hand extended, the woman
with the one leg crossed,

sticking out. Now the handsome
one walks off, business
completed. Time to go.

    .

If you could look
as good as you could
look, you surely would.

    .

Eyes

Tall
dark
woman

with
black, wide,
shadowed eyes.

.

Great
shade of orange.

.

I don't do this
for nothing yet.

.

Hours
pass.

.

Here

Sounds like ball
in bowling alley.

Music's
underneath it.

Clapped
hands.

Hums
of various conversations,

people sitting out
on couches,

wide,
low ceilinged space.

Kimonoed kid
sits on floor with buddy.

　　·

Three.
Straight up.

　　·

Each one
trying to stay someone.

En Route San Francisco

Say Something

Say something
to me. "Could you
help me with
this . . ." Such

possibly the woman's
(Thailand) speech
in aisle adjacent,
plane's body, going

through night. It's
going home, with me—
months passed,
things happened in.

I need some
summary, gloss
of it all, days
later. Last recall

was Bobbie in
the kitchen saying
apropos coat, "If
you don't wear it

now, you never will . . ."
Or Bobbie, at airport,
re people—
"They all look

like R. Crumb
characters . . ." It
drifts, it
stays by itself.

      •

Friends I've loved
all the time,
Joanne,
Shao—but

not so
simply
now
to name them.

      •

I could get drunker
and wiser
and lower
and higher.

.

Peter's
amulet
worked!

.

Kyoto

"Arthur's friend's
a nice man!"

.

Memory

Nancy finally
at the kitchen table.

.

Bobbie

Her voice,
her voice, her
lovely voice . . .

    .

Now's
the time.

    .

Watching water
blast up
on window
Provincetown—

clouds, air, trees,
ground,
watching for
the next one.

    .

One's so neat
about it.

    .

Echo

Faint, persistent
smell of shit.

    .

Mommy

Kid's been crying
so long.

    ·

If You're Going to Have One

The Chinese, Koreans,
Filipinos, persons from
Thailand

"are better fathers and mothers."

    ·

On Board

The mommy,
daddy

number.

    ·

God a
crying
kid.

    ·

Later

It feels things
are muddled again
when I wanted
my head straight—

in this empty place,
people sleeping, light
from another person
reading lets me see.

That's talking about it.
This is—this is
where I've been before
and now don't want to go back to.

    ·

No blaming anyone,
nothing I can't do,
nowhere to be happy
but where I am.

    ·

Plans—the next
six months
all arranged.

    ·

You can see her face,
hear her voice,
hope it's happy.

5/3

A Note

To move in such fashion through nine countries (Fiji was my first stop, so to speak) in a little over two months is a peculiarly American circumstance, and the record thus provoked is *personal* in a manner not only the effect of my own egocentricity, but, again, a fact of American social reality. The tourist will always be singular, no matter what the occasion otherwise—and there is a sense, I think, in which Americans still presume the world as something to look at and use, rather than to live in. Again and again, I found that other cultural patterns, be they Samoan, Chinese, Malaysian, or Filipino, could not easily think of one as singular, and such familiar concepts as the "nuclear family" or "alienation" had literally to be translated for them. Whereas our habit of social value constantly promotes an isolation—the house in the country, the children in good schools—theirs, of necessity, finds center and strength in the collective, unless it has been perverted by Western exploitation and greed.

Not long ago, reading poems at a communal center in Indianapolis, I was asked by a member of the black community to explain my going to such places as the Philippines and South Korea—where overtly fascist governments are in power—sponsored by our State Department. The same question was put to me by an old friend indeed, Cid Corman, in Kyoto. How could I answer? That I am American? That the government is mine too? I wish I might find so simply a vindication. No, I went because I wanted to—to look, to see, even so briefly, how people in those parts of the world made a reality, to talk of being American, of the past war, of power, of usual life in this country, of my fellow and sister poets, of my neighbors on Fargo Street in Buffalo, New York. I wanted, at last, to be *human,* however simplistic that wish. I took thus my own chances, and remarkably found a company. My deepest thanks to them all.

—R. C.

Later

Count then your blessings, hold in mind
All that has loved you or been kind . . .
Gather the bits of road that were
Not gravel to the traveller
But eternal lanes of joy
On which no man who walks can die.

— FROM PATRICK KAVANAGH, "PRELUDE"

One

Myself

What, younger, felt
was possible, now knows
is not—but still
not changed enough—

Walked by the sea,
unchanged in memory—
evening, as clouds
on the far-off rim

of water float,
pictures of time,
smoke, faintness—
still the dream.

I want, if older,
still to know
why, human, men
and women are

so torn, so lost,
why hopes cannot
find better world
than this.

Shelley is dead and gone,
who said,
"Taught them not this—
to know themselves;

their might Could not repress
the mutiny within,
And for the morn
of truth they feigned,

deep night
Caught them ere evening . . ."

This World

If night's the harder,
closer time, days
come. The morning
opens with light

at the window.
Then, as now, sun
climbs in blue sky.
At noon

on the beach
I could watch
these glittering
waves forever,

follow their sound
deep into mind
and echoes —
let light

as air
be relief.
The wind
pulls at face

and hands,
grows cold. What
can one think—
the beach

is myriad stone.
Clouds pass,
grey undersides,
white clusters

of air, all
air. Water
moves at the edges,
blue, green,

white twists
of foam.
What then
will be lost,

recovered.
What
matters as one
in this world?

The House

Mas-Soñer
Restaurat—Any—
1920 . . . Old
slope of roof,

gutted windows,
doors, the walls,
with crumbling stucco
shows the mortar

and stones
underneath. Sit
on stone wall adjacent
topped with brick,

ground roundabout's weeds,
red dirt, bare rock.
Then look east
down through valley—

fruit trees in their rows,
the careful fields,
the tops of the other
farmhouses below—

then the city, in haze,
the sea. Look
back in time
if you can—

think of the
myriad people
contained in this instant
in mind. But the well

top's gone, and debris
litters entrance.
Yet no sadness,
no fears

life's gone out.
Could put it all right,
given time,
and need, and money,

make this place sing,
the rooms open
and warm, and spring
come in at the windows

with the breeze—
the white blossom
of apple
still make this song.

La Conca

Sand here's like meal—
oats, barley, or wheat—
feels round and specific.

Sun's hot,
just past noon, and sound
of small boat clearing headland

chugs against wash.
Light slants
now on rocks, makes shadows.

Beach is a half-moon's
curve, with bluff,
at far end, of rock—

and firs look like garden
so sharply their tops
make line against sky.

All quiet here,
all small
and comfortable. Boat goes by,

beyond, where sky
and sea meet
far away.

Sea

Ever
to sleep,
returning water.

.

Rock's upright,
thinking.

.

Boy and dog
following
the edge.

.

Come back, first
wave I saw.

.

Older man at
water's edge, brown
pants rolled up,
white legs, and hair.

.

Thin faint
clouds begin
to drift over
sun, im-
perceptibly.

    .

Stick stuck
in sand, shoes,
sweater, cigarettes.

    .

No home more
to go to.

    .

But that line,
sky and sea's,
something else.

    .

Adios, water—
for another day.

Flaubert's Early Prose

"Eventually he dies
out of a lack of will to live,
out of mere weariness and sadness . . ."

And then he is hit by a truck
on his way home from work,

and/or a boulder
pushed down onto him
by lifelong friends of the family
writes FINIS to his suffering—

Or he goes to college,
gets married,
and *then* he dies!

Or finally he doesn't die at all,
just goes on living,
day after day in the same old way . . .

He is a very interesting man,
this intensively sensitive person,
but he has to die somehow—

so he goes by himself to the beach,
and sits down and thinks,
looking at the water to be found there,

"Why was I born? Why
am I living?"—like
an old song, *cheri*—
and then he dies.

Barcelona: February 13, 1977

Grave, to the will
of the people,
in the plaza
in front of the cathedral,
at noon dance
the *sardana*—

"two policemen dead,
four arrested" –

ritual, formal,
grave, old and young,
coats left in heap
in the middle
of the circle, wind chill –
dance, to find will.

Place

This is an empty landscape,
in spite of its light,
air, water –
the people walking the streets.

I feel faint here,
too far off, too
enclosed in myself,
can't make love a way out.

I need the old-time density,
the dirt, the cold,
the noise through the floor –
my love in company.

Speech

Simple things
one wants to say
like, what's the day
like, out there—
who am I
and where.

Beach

Across bay's loop
of whitecaps,
small seeming black
figures at edge—

one, the smallest,
to the water goes.
Others, behind,
sit down.

After

I'll not write again
things a young man
thinks, not the words
of that feeling.

There is no world
except felt, no
one there but
must be here also.

If that time was
echoing, a vindication
apparent, if flesh
and bone coincided—

let the body be.
See faces float
over the horizon let
the day end.

For Pen

Reading, in the chair
in front of the fire
keeps the room both warm
and sparely human—

thinking, to where I've come,
where come from,
from what, from whom—
wanting a meaning.

None to hand but the days
pass here,
in dear company
takes mind of shy comfort.

I want the world
I did always,
small pieces
and clear acknowledgments.

I want to be useful
to someone, I think,
always—if not many,
then one.

But to have it
be echo, feeling
that was years ago—
now my hands are

wrinkled and my hair
goes grey—seems
ugly burden
and mistake of it.

So sing this
weather, passing,
grey and blue
together, rain and sun.

Love

There are words voluptuous
as the flesh
in its moisture,
its warmth.

Tangible, they tell
the reassurances,
the comforts,
of being human.

Not to speak them
makes abstract
all desire
and its death at last.

Erotica

On the path
down here, to the sea,
there are bits

of pages
from a magazine, scattered,
the *big tits*

of my adolescence
caught on bushes,
stepped on, faces

of the women, naked,
still smiling out at me
from the grass.

In the factory,
beside which
this path goes,

there is
no one. The windows
are broken out.

A dump
sits in front of it.
Two piles of dirt

beyond that.
Do these
look like tits

too, some primordial
woman sunk
underground

breaking out,
up,
to get me—

shall I throw
myself down
upon it,

this ground
rolls and twists,
these pictures

I want still
to see. Coming back
a day later,

kids were stopped
at that spot
to look

as I would
and had—there the fact
of the mystery

at last—
"what they look like
underneath"—

paper shreds,
blurred pages,
dirty pictures.

Nature

FOR R. B. K.

Out door here—
tall as wall
of usual room,
slight arch at top—

sunlight
in courtyard
beyond
settles on stump

of tree's trunk—
limbs all cut
to force growth,
come summer—

in blue and white
checkerboard tiled
square planter
at bottom

sits in cement,
thoughtful,
men's minded
complement.

Thinking of Walter Benjamin

What to say
these days
of crashing disjunct,
whine, of separation—

Not abstract—
"God's will," not
lost in clouds this
experienced wisdom.

Hand and mind
and heart one
ground to walk on,
field to plow.

I know
a story
I can tell
and will.

Waiting for a Bus "En Frente de la Iglesia"

Here's the church,
here's the tower, the wall,
chopped off. *Open*

*the door—*no
people. This is
age, long time gone,

like town gate sits
at intersection
across—just façade

leading nowhere.
Zipzap, the cars
roar past. Three

faded flags flap
on top of Hotel
Florida. Old dog,

old friend, walks toward us,
legs rachitic, stiff,
reddish hair all fuzzed.

Long grey bus
still parked to go
to Gerona

which, 8th century,
Charlemagne came personally
to take back from Moors.

You can *read*
all about it!
but wind's cold

in this early spring sun,
and this bench's
lost its bars

on the back
but for one—
and bus

now starts up,
and we're on,
and we're gone.

News of the World

Topical questions,
as the world swirls,
and never

enough in hand,
head, to know
if Amin

will truly become
"Jimmy Carter's best friend"
as he professes. The facts

are literal daily horror:
$1/5$ of world's population has no access
to processed drinking water;

"women in rural Burma
walk 15 miles a day to get some
and bring it home,
a six hour trip." Or

Romania's earthquake dead—
"What day is today
and how are my parents?"

were the first words of Sorin Crainic
when he emerged from the rubble
after eleven days. "I kept

hoping all the time.
My hope has come true.
I shall be able to walk again

and breathe fresh air, much
fresh air.
I shall go back to work."

Meanwhile, same page, "Goldwater
Denounces Report Linking Him
To Gang Figures"—"A 36-member

team of journalists from 23 newspapers
and broadcast outlets . . . continuing
work begun by reporter Don Bolles . . .

who was murdered last June. One man
has pleaded guilty to second-degree
murder in the killing; two

are awaiting trial." G. believes
"that the reporters had gone to Arizona
hoping to solve the Bolles murder"

but when "they could not" did
"a job" on said state. Too late,
too little. But not for you, Mr. G.,

as hate grows, lies, the same
investment of the nice and tidy
ways to get "rich,"

in this "world,"
wer eld, the length
of a human life.

Morning

Shadows, on the far wall,
of courtyard, from the sun
back of house, faint

traceries, of the leaves,
the arch of the balcony —
greens, faded white,

high space of flat
blind-sided building
sits opposite this

window, in high door,
across the floor here
from this table

where I'm sitting, writing,
feet on cold floor's
tiles, watching this light.

The Table

Two weeks from now
we'll be gone. Think,
problems will be
over, the time here

done. What's the time
left to be.
Sky's grey again,
electric stove whirs

by the wall with its
snowflake, flowerlike
yellow, blue and green
tile design. On the table

the iris have opened,
two wither and close.
Small jug holds them,
green stalks, husks and buds.

Paper, yesterday's, book
to read face down, ashtray,
cigarettes, letter from
your mother, roll now

of thunder outside. You
put down the papers,
go back to reading
your book, head bent.

Sarah's cap on your hair
holds it close—red at top,
in a circle, first ring French
blue, then one lighter,

then the darker repeated.
Think of the sounds,
outside, now quiet,
the kids gone back to school.

It's a day we may
live forever, this
simple one. Nothing
more, nothing less.

Childish

Great stories matter—
but the one who tells them
hands them on
in turn to another

who also will.
What's in the world
is water, earth,
and fire, some people,

animals, trees, birds,
etc. I can see
as far as you,
and what I see I tell

as you told me
or have or will.
You'll see too
as well.

Echoes

Eight panes
in this window
for God's light,
for the outside,

comes through door
this morning.
Sun makes laced
shadows on wall

through imperfect glass.
Mind follows,
finds the lines,
the wavering places.

Rest wants
to lie down
in the sun,
make resolution.

Body sits single,
waiting—
but for what
it knows not.

Old words
echoing what
the physical
can't—

"Leave love,
leave day,
come
with me."

Reflections

What pomposity
could say only—
Look
at what's happened to me.

All those others
surrounding
know
the same bounds.

Happiness
finds itself
in one or many
the same—

and dead,
no more than one
or less
makes a difference.

I was thinking
this morning
again—
So be it.

New Moon

Are there still some
"quiet craters of the moon" –
seeing that edge of it
you were pointing to,

stopped, in the street,
looking past the wires
on those poles, all
the stores, open, people,

cars, going past, to see
in that space, faint sliver
of its visible edge. What
advice then remembered,

what had she said?
*Turn your money over
and bow three times
to make it increase.*

Later

If I could get
my hands on
a little bit
of it – neither fish,

flesh, nor fowl. Not
you, Harry. No one's
mother – or father,
or children. Not

me again. Not
earth, sky, water—
no mind, no time.
No islands in the sun.

Money I don't want.
No place more
than another—
I'm not here

by myself. But,
if you want to give
me something for Xmas,
I'll be around.

Night Time

When the light leaves
and sky's black,
no nothing
to look at,

day's done.
That's it.

Peace

You're looking at a chopper,
brother—no words to say.
Just step on
the gas, man, up and away.

That's dead, I know,
I don't even talk like that
any more. My teeth
are hurting.

But if you'll wait
out back, and
hit yourself over the head
with a hard object,

you'll dig, like, you
like me were young once,
jesus, here come
the creeps. I wrote

a book once, and was
in love with
substantial objects.
No more, I can

get out of here
or come here
or go there
or here, in five minutes.

Later. This
is just to say I was
something or other, and you dig it,
that's it, brother.

Blues

FOR TOM PICKARD

Old-time blues
and things to say—
not going home
till they come to get me.

See the sky
black as night,
drink what's
there to drink.

God's dead,
men take over,
world's round,
all over.

Think of it,
all those years,
no one's the wiser
even older.

Flesh, flesh,
screams in body,
you know,
got to sleep.

Got to eat, baby,
got to.
No way
you won't.

When I lay down
big bed
going to pillow
my sleeping head.

When I fall,
I fall,
straight down deep
I'm going.

No one
touch me
with
their doubting mind.

You don't
love me
like you
say you do, you

don't do me
like you
said
you would.

What I say
to people
don't mean
I don't love,

what I
do don't
do, don't don't
do enough.

Think I drink
this little glass,
sit on my ass,
think about

life, all
those things,
substance.
I could touch you.

Times in jail
I was scared
not of being hurt
but that people lock you up,

what's got to be
cruel is you know,
and I don't, you say
you got the truth.

I wouldn't listen
if I was drunk, couldn't hear
if I was stoned,
you tell me right or don't.

Come on home, brother,
you make a fool,
get in trouble, end up
in jail.

I'm in the jailhouse now.
When they lock the door,
how long is what
you think of.

Believe in what's there,
nowhere else it will be.
They kill you,
they kill me.

Both dead,
we'll rise again.
They believe in Christ,
they'll believe in men.

Spring in San Feliu

Think of the good times—
again. Can't let it all
fail, fall apart, at
that always vague edge is

the public so-called condition,
which nobody knows enough
ever, even those
are supposed to be it.

I could identify that man,
say, bummed us out, or
the woman took the whole
street to walk in. They are

familiar faces, anywhere. They
don't need a place. But,
quieter, the kid took the running
leap past us, to show off,

the one then asked to look in
to the courtyard, saw the house,
said, *que casa grande!,* sans malice
or envy, the ones let us off

the hook of the randomly purposive
traveler, the dogs that
came with us, over hill,
over dale, the country men and women

could look up from those
rows of stuff they had planted,
showed now green, in the sun,
—how modest those farms and those lives.

Well, walk on . . . We'll be gone
soon enough. I'll have got
all I wanted—your time and your love
and yourself—like, *poco a poco.*

That sea never cared about us.
Nor those rocks nor those hills,
nor the far-off mountains still
white with snow. The sun

came with springtime—*la
primavera,* they'll say, when
we've gone. But we came.
We've been here.

4/1/77

Sparrows

Small birds fly up
shaft of stairwell,

sit, chirping,
where sun strikes in at top.

Last time we'll see them,
hear their feisty greeting

to the day's first light,
the coming of each night.

End

End of page,
end of this

company — wee
notebook kept

my mind in hand,
let the world stay

open to me
day after day,

words to say,
things to be.

Two

For John Chamberlain

They paid my way here
and I'll get myself home.
Old saying:
Let the good times roll.

. . .

This is Austin
spelled with an H? This is
Houston, Texas—
Houston Street is back there—

ways in and out
of New York. The billboards
are better than the natural view,
you dig. I came here

just to see you, personal
as God and just as real.
I may never go home
again. Meantime

the lead room with the x
number of people
under the street
is probably empty tonight.

In New York, in
some other place.
Many forms.
Many farms, ranches

in Texas—many places,
many miles, big
endless spaces they say.
This is Marlboro Country

with box those dimensions,
module. Old movie of you
using baler with the crunchers
coming down so delicately.

The kids in the loft, long space.
The Oldenbergs going to work,
eight o'clock. Viva
talking and talking. Now I'm

stoned again, I was
stoned again, all that
past, years
also insistent dimension.

If I could take the world,
and put it on its side, man,
and squeeze just in the right
places. Wow. I don't think

much of interest would happen.
Like the lion coming into the room
with two heads, we'd all end up
killing it to see it.

So this is Art and here we are.
Who would have thought it?
I'll go sooner than you.
I can always tell

no matter how long I sit
after they've all gone, but the bottle
isn't empty.
No one's going to throw me out.

Let's sit in a bar and cry again.
Fuck it! Let's go out on your boat
and I'll fall asleep just like
they all do you tell me.

Terrific. Water's
an obvious material.
You could even make
a suit out of it. You could

do anything you wanted to,
possibly, if you wanted to.
Like coming through customs
with the grey leather hat.

It's all so serious and wonderful.
It's all so big and small.
Upended, it begins again, all the way
from the end to the very beginning,

again. I want it two ways,
she said, in a book
someone wrote. I want it all.
I want to take it all home.

But there's too much already
of everything, and something
I have to let go
and that's me, here and now.

But before leaving, may I say
that you are a great artist
whatever that turns out to be,
and art is art because of you.

I Love You

I see you, Aunt Bernice—
and your smile anticipating reality.
I don't care any longer that you're older.
There are times all the time the same.

I'm a young old man here on earth,
sticks, dust, rain, trees, people.
Your cat killing rats in Florida was incredible—
Pete—weird, sweet presence. Strong.

You were good to me. You had *wit*—
value beyond all other human possibility.
You could smile at the kids, the old cars.
Your house in N.H. was lovely.

Four Years Later

When my mother
died, her things were
distributed

so quickly. Nothing
harsh about it,
just gone,

it seemed, but
for small
mementos, pictures

of family, dresses,
a sweater,
clock.

Looking back
now, wish
I'd talked

more to her.
I tried
in the hospital

but our habit
was too deep—
we didn't

speak easily.
Sitting
now, here,

early morning,
by myself,
can hear her—

as, "Bob,
do what you have to—
I trust you—"

words like
"presumption," possibly
"discretion"—some

insistent demand to
cover living
with clothes—not

"dressed up" but
common, faithful—
what no other can know.

Heaven

If life were easy
and it all worked out,
what would this sadness
be about.

If it was happy
day after day,
what would happen
anyway.

Neighbors

Small horses on windowsill
adjacent, 'cross street,
kid's apparent

window, three point
one way, one
another, to face

babydoll, sits there,
with curtains drawn.
Everyone's gone.

July: Fargo Street

Bangs in street.
Fourth's here again,
200th yet,

useless as ever,
'cept for energies
of kids, and the

respite from work
for all these
surrounding neighbors.

Thinking of Yeats

Break down
"innocence"—
tell truth,

be *small*
in world's
wilderness.

P—

Swim
on her
as in
an ocean.

    ·

Think out
of it—

be here.

    ·

Hair's
all around,

floats
in flesh.

    ·

Eyes'
measure,

mouth's small
discretion.

Smiles.

.

Long warmth,
speaks

too.

.

Couldn't
do it
better.

.

Can walk
along.

Blue Skies Motel

Look at
that motherfucking smokestack

pointing
straight up.

See those clouds,
old-time fleecy pillows,

like they say, whites and greys,
float by.

There's cars
on the street,

there's a swimming pool
out front—

and the trees
go yellow

now
it's the fall.

Riddle

What'd you throw it on the floor for?
Who the hell you think you are

come in here
push me around.

For Pen

Thinking out
of the heart—

it's up,
it's down . . .

It's that time
of day light

echoes the sun
setting west

over mountains.
I want to come home.

Ciano's

Walking
off street

into Ciano's—
last sun

yellow
through door.

The bar
an oval, people—

behind is
pool table.

Sitting
and thinking.

Dreaming
again

of blue eyes,
actually green—

whose head's
red, mouth's

round, soft
sounds—

whose waist is
an arrow

points down
to earth.

Train Going By

FOR ROSALIE SORRELS

When I was a kid
I wanted to get educated
and to college go
to learn how to know.

Now old I've found
train going by
will take me along
but I still don't know why.

Not just for money
not for love
not for anything thought
for nothing I've done—

it's got to be luck
keeps the world going round
myself moving on
on that train going by.

For Pen

Last day of year,
sky's a light

open grey, blue
spaces appear

in lateral tiers.
Snow's fallen,

will again. Morning
sounds hum, inside,

outside, roosters squawk,
dog barks, birds squeak.

—"Be happy with me."

Loner

Sounds, crank
of kid's cart's axle

on street, one
floor down.

Heat's thick,
sun's bright

in window still
early morning,

May, fifty-first
birthday. What

time will the
car be done, time—

ready? Sits opposite,
love, in red wrapper,

sheen of silk,
sideways, hair, hands,

breasts, young
flight of fancy,

long fingers, here
in a way

wants the dream back,
keeps walking.

B. B.

What's gone,
bugger all—

nothing lost
in mind till

it's all
forgotten.

Morning

Light's bright glimmer,
through green bottle

on shelf
above. Light's white

fair air,
shimmer,

blue summer's
come.

Thanks

Here's to Eddie—
not unsteady
when drunk,
just thoughtful.

Here's to his mind
can remember
in the blur
his own forgotten line.

Or, too, lest
forgot, him in the traffic
at Cambridge, outside,
lurching, confident.

He told me later,
"I'm Catholic,
I'm queer,
I'm a poet."

God bless him,
God love him,
I say,
praise him

who saves you time,
saves you money,
takes on the burden
of your own confessions.

And my thanks again
for the cigarettes
he gave me
someone else had left.

I won't escape
his conversation
but will listen
as I've learned to,

and drink
and think again
with this dear man
of the true, the good, the dead.

Theresa's Friends

From the outset
charmed by the soft, quick speech
of those men and women,
Theresa's friends—and the church

she went to, the "other,"
not the white plain Baptist
I tried to learn God in.
Or, later, in Boston the legend

of "being Irish," the lore, the magic,
the violence, the comfortable
or uncomfortable drunkenness.
But most, that endlessly present talking,

as Mr. Connealy's, the ironmonger,
sat so patient in Cronin's Bar,
and told me sad, emotional stories
with the quiet air of an elder

does talk to a younger man.
Then, when at last I was twenty-one,
my mother finally told me
indeed the name *Creeley* was Irish—

and the heavens opened, birds sang,
and the trees and the ladies spoke
with wondrous voices. The power of the glory
of poetry—was at last mine.

Later

1
Shan't be winding
back in blue
gone time ridiculous,
nor lonely

anymore. Gone,
gone—wee thin
delights, hands
held me, mouths

winked with white
clean teeth. Those
clothes have fluttered
their last regard

to this passing
person walks by
that flat back-
yard once and for all.

2
You won't want to be early
for passage of grey mist
now rising from the faint

river alongside the childhood
fields. School bell rings,
to bring you all in again.

That's mother sitting there,
a father dead in heaven,
a dog barks, steam of

drying mittens on the stove,
blue hands, two doughnuts
on a plate.

3
The small
spaces of existence,
sudden

smell of burning
leaves makes
place in time

these days
(these days)
passing,

common
to one
and all.

4
Opening
the boxes packed
in the shed,

at the edge
of the porch
was to be

place to sit
in the sun,
glassed over,

in the winter
for looking out
to the west,

see the shadows
in the early
morning lengthen,

sharp cold
dryness of air,
sounds of cars,

dogs, neighbors,
persons
of house, toilet

flush, pan
rattle, door
open, never done.

5
Eloquent,
my heart,

thump bump —
My Funny Valentine

6
If you saw
dog pass, in car —

looking out, possibly
indifferently, at you —

would you — *could* you —
shout, "Hey, Spot!

It's me!" After all
these years,

no dog's coming home
again. Its skin's

moldered
through rain, dirt,

to dust, hair alone
survives, matted tangle.

Your own, changed,
your hair, greyed,

your voice not the one
used to call him home,

"Hey Spot!" *The world's
greatest dog*'s got

lost in the world,
got lost long ago.

7
Oh sadness,
boring

preoccupation —
rain's wet,

clouds
pass.

8
Nothing "late" about the
"no place to go" old folks —

or "hell," or
"Florida this winter."

No "past" to be
inspired by "futures,"

scales of the imperium,
wonders of what's next.

When I was a kid, I
thought like a kid —

I *was* a kid,
you dig it. But

a hundred and fifty years later,
that's a whole long time to

wait for the train.
No doubt West Acton

was improved by the discontinuance
of service, the depot taken down,

the hangers-around there moved
at least back a street to Mac's Garage.

And you'll have to drive your own car
to get to Boston – or take the bus.

These days, call it "last Tuesday,"
1887, my mother was born,

and now, sad to say,
she's dead. And especially "you"

can't argue
with the facts.

9
Sitting up here in
newly constituted

attic room 'mid
pipes, scarred walls,

the battered window
adjacent looks out

to street below. It's fall,
sign woven in iron

rails of neighbor's porch:
"Elect Pat Sole."

O sole mio, mother,
thinking of old attic,

West Acton farmhouse,
same treasures here, the boxes,

old carpets, the smell.
On wall facing, in chalk:

KISS ME. *I love you.*
Small world of these pinnacles,

places ride up in these
houses like clouds,

and I've come as far,
as high, as I'll go.

Sweet weather,
turn now of year . . .

The old horse chestnut,
with trunk a stalk like a flower's,

gathers strength to face winter.
The spiked pods of its seeds

start to split, soon will drop.
The patience, of small lawns, small hedges,

papers blown by the wind,
the light fading, gives way

to the season. School's
started again. Footsteps fall

on sidewalk down three
stories. It's man-made

endurance I'm after,
it's love for the wear

and the tear here,
goes under, gets broken, but stays.

Where finally else
in the world come to rest—

by a brook, by a
view with a farm

like a dream—in
a forest? In a house

has walls all around it?
There's more always here

than just me, in this room,
this attic, apartment,

this house, this world,
can't escape.

10
In testament
to a willingness

to *live,* I,
Robert Creeley,

being of sound body
and mind, admit

to other preoccupations—
with the future, with

the past. But now—
but now the wonder of life is

that *it is* at all,
this sticky sentimental

warm enclosure,
feels place in the physical

with others,
lets mind wander

to wondering thought,
then lets go of itself,

finds a home
on earth.

> *— 400 Fargo*
> *Buffalo, N.Y.*
> *Sept. 3rd – 13th, 1977 —*

For Rene Ricard

Remote control factors
of existence, like
"I wanted it this way!"

And hence to Lenox
one summer's day
with old friend, Warren Tallman,

past charming hills
and valleys give class
to that part of western Mass.

I can get funny —
and I can get lost,
go wandering on,

with friends like signboards
flashing past
in those dark nights of the soul.

All one world, Rene,
no matter one's half
of all it is or was.

So walking with you and Pepi,
talking, gossiping,
thank god—the useful news—

what's presently the word
of X, Y, and Z
in NYC, the breezes

on the hill, by the orchard
where Neil sits under tree,
blow the words away,

while he watches me talk,
mouth poems for them,
though he can't hear a word.

This is art,
the public act
that all those dirt roads lead to,

all those fucking bogs
and blown-out tires
and broken fan belts—

willed decision—
call it,
though one's too dumb to know.

For me—and possibly
for only me—a bird
sits in a lousy tree,

and sings and sings
all goddamn day,
and what I do

is write it down,
in words
they call them:

him, and *it,* and *her,*
some story this
will sometimes tell

or not. The bird
can't care, the
tree can hardly hold it up —

and me is least of all
its worry. What then
is this life all about.

Simple. It's garbage
dumped in street,
a friend's quick care,

someone who hates you
and won't go way,
a breeze

blowing past Neil's
malfunctioning dear ears,
a blown-out dusty room,

an empty echoing kitchen,
a physical heart
which goes or stops.

For you—
because you carry wit with you,
and you are there somehow

at the hard real times,
and you know them too—
a necessary love.

The Place

... Swoop of hawk—
or mind's adjustment

to sight—*memory?*
Air unrelieved, *unlived?*

Begun again, begin
again the play

of cloud, the lift
of sudden cliff,

the place in place—
the way it was again.

Go back a day,
take everything, take time

and play it back
again, the staggering

path, ridiculous, uncertain
bird, blurred, fuzzy

fog—or rocks which
seem to hang in

imperceptible substance
there, or here,

in thought? This thinking
is a place itself

unthought, which comes
to be the world.

Learning

"Suggestion/recognition . . ."
The horse
at the edge of the pool,

or the horse's ass,
the fool,
either end, sits

waiting for world
to resolve it—
Or in swirl

of these apparent facts,
contexts, states,
of possible being,

among all others,
of numbered time,
one or two

gleam clearly
there, now *here*—
in mind.

Corn Close

FOR BASIL BUNTING

Words again, rehearsal—
"Are we going
to get up *into*

heaven—after all?"
What's
the sound of *that,*

who, where—
and how.
One wonder,

one wonders, sees
the world—
specifically, this one.

Sheep, many
with lambs,
of a spring morning,

on sharp slope of hill's side,
run up it
in chill rain.

Below's brook,
as I'd say,
a *burn?* a *beck?*

Goddamnit, *learn* it.
Fell fills eye,
as we lie abed.

Basil's up and out
walking
with the weather's

vagaries. His home is
this world's
wetness

or any's, feet
planted on ground,
and but

for trash can takes
weekly hauling
up and down,

no seeming fact
of age presently
bothers him.

Vague palaver.
Can I get the fire
to burn with wet wood?

Am I useful
today? Will I fuck up
the fireplace?

Drop
log
on my foot.

At breakfast we sit,
provided, tea's steam,
hot scones, butter,

marmalade—Basil's
incurious, reassuring
smile—*and* stories

of Queen E's
garden party, the thousands
jammed into garden—

style
of a damned poor
sort . . . Consider

(at night) Corelli
gives lifetime
to getting it right:

the *Twelve Concerti Grossi,*
not Ives
(whom I love),

not makeshift,
tonal blather—
but sound meets sound

with clear edge,
finds place,
precise, in the mind.

Have you seen a hawk—
look out! It
will get you,

blurred,
patient person,
drinking, eating,

sans body, sans
history, in-
telligence, etc.

Oh, I think
the words come from
the world and go

"I know
not
where . . ."

Their breasts banging—
flap—on their breastbones
makes the dear *sound*—

like tire tread
pulled from the shoe—
flap flap, bangs the body,

chortles, gurgles,
wheezes, breathes,
"Camptown race is (?)

five miles long!"
Back on the track,
you asshole.

No excuses,
no
"other things to do"—

And Wyatt's
flight through the night
is an honest

apprehension:
They *flee*
from *me*

that sometime did me seek ...
When we'd first come,
our thought

was to help him,
old friend, and brought
such scanty makeshift

provision, in retrospect
I blush—as who
would give to Northumbrian

Teacher's
as against Glenfiddich—
which he had.

Was I scared
old friend
would be broken

by world
all his life
had lived in,

or that art,
his luck,
had gone sour?

My fear
is my own.
He got

the car started
after I tried
and tried, felt

battery fading,
mist-sodden spark plugs—
despair!

He had a wee can
in his hand,
and he sprayed

minute part
of its contents—
phfft!—on car's motor,

and car starts,
by god. What wonder
more than

to be where you are,
and to know it?
All's here.

The Children

AFTER PATRICK KAVANAGH

Down on the sidewalk recurrent
children's forms, reds, greens,
walking along with the watching
elders not their own.

It's winter, grows colder and colder.
How to play today without sun?
Will summer, gone, come again?
Will I only grow older and older?

Not wise enough yet to know
you're only here at all
as the wind blows, now
as the fire burns low.

Three

Desultory Days

FOR PETER WARSHALL

Desultory days,
time's wandering
impermanences—

like, *what's for lunch,*
Mabel? Hunks
of unwilling

meat got chopped
from recalcitrant
beasts? "No tears

for this vision"—
nor huge strawberries
zapped from forlorn Texas,

too soon, too soon . . .
We will meet again
one day, we will

gather at the river
(Paterson perchance)
so turgidly oozes by,

etc. Nothing new in the world
but us, the human
parasite eats up

that self-defined reality
we talked about in
ages past. Now prophecy declares,

got to get on with it,
back to the farm, else die
in streets inhuman

'spite we made them every one.
Ah friends, before I die,
I want to sit awhile

upon this old world's knee,
yon charming hill, you see,
and dig the ambient breezes,

make of life
such gentle passing pleasure!
Were it then wrong

to avoid, as might be said,
the heaped-up canyons of the dead—
L.A.'s drear smut, and N.Y.C.'s

crunched millions? I don't know.
It seems to me
what can salvation be

for less than 1%
of so-called population
is somehow latent fascism

of the soul. What leaves behind
those other people,
like they say,

reneges on Walter Whitman's
19th century Mr. Goodheart's
Lazy Days and Ways In Which

we might still *save the world.*
I loved it but
I never could believe it—

rather, the existential
terror of New England
countrywoman, Ms.

Dickinson: "The Brain, within its Groove
Runs evenly—and true—
But let a Splinter swerve—

"'Twere easier for You—//
To put a Current back—
When Floods have slit the Hills—

"And scooped a Turnpike for Themselves—
And Trodden out the Mills—"
moves me. My mind

to me a nightmare is—
that thought of days,
years, went its apparent way

without itself, with
no other company than thought.
So—*born to die*—why

take everything with us?
Why the meagerness
of life deliberately,

why the patience
when of no use,
and the anger, when it is?

I am no longer
one man—
but an old one

who is human again
after a long time,
feels the meat contract,

or stretch, upon bones,
hates to be alone
but can't stand interruption.

Funny
how it all works out,
and Asia is

after all *how much money
it costs—*
either to buy or to sell it.

Didn't they have a
world too? But then
they don't look like us,

do they? But they'll get us,
someone will—they'll find us,
they won't leave us here

just to die
by ourselves
all alone?

Arroyo

Out the window,
across the ground there,
persons walk
in the hard sun—

Like years ago we'd watch
the children go to school
in the vacant building now
across the arroyo.

Same persons,
Mr. Gutierrez and,
presumably, his son,
Victor, back from the army—

Would wave to me
if I did to them,
call *que tal, hello,*
across the arroyo.

How sentimental,
heartfelt, this life becomes
when you try to think of it,
say it in simple words—

How far in time and space
the distance,
the simple division of a ditch,
between people.

For John Duff

"I placed a jar in Tennessee . . ."

– WALLACE STEVENS, "ANECDOTE OF THE JAR"

Blast of harsh
flat sunlight

on recalcitrant ground
after rain. Ok.

Life in N.M. is
not a tourist's paradise,

not the solar
energy capital

of the world, not
your place in the sun. If

I had my way,
I'd be no doubt

long gone. But
here I am and we talk

of plastic America,
of other friends

other places. What
will we do

today. When
will heart's peace

descend in rippling, convenient
waves. Why

is the sky still
so high.

What's
underfoot.

I don't
feel comfortable with Indians—

and the Mexican
neighbors with

seventeen kids—
what time exists

now still to
include them.

Ok. A day
goes by. Night

follows. On the slight
lip of earth

down from the gate
at the edge of

the arroyo
sits

a *menhir*—
remember

that oar
you could screw into

ground, say,
here I'll build a city?

No way.
This column

is common
old stretcher

cement blocks.
Put one on one

in pairs, first this way,
then that, you get

a house,
explicit, of the mind,

both thought
and the senses provoke it—

you see it—
you feel and think

this world.
It's a quiet

grey column,
handsome—"the one

missing color"—
and it's here now

forever,
no matter

it falls in a day.
Ok, John.

When you're gone,
I'll remember

also forever
the tough dear

sentiment, the clarity,
of your talking, the care.

And this *it*
you gave us:

here
is all the wonder,

there
is all there is.

Talk

One thing, strikes in,
recall, anyone talking
got to be to human

or something, like a rock,
a "song," a thing to
talk to, to talk to.

Poor

Nothing's
today and
tomorrow only.

    ·

Slow-
er.

    ·

Place-
ss.

       •

POOR
Pur-
pose por-
puss.

       •

Sore hand.

       •

Got
to get going.

       •

And I was
not asleep

and I was
not alone.

Touchstone

FOR L. Z.

"Something
by which
all else
can be measured."

Something
by which
to measure
all else.

Morning (8:10 AM)

In sun's
slow rising
this morning

antenna tower
catches
the first light,

shines
for an instant
silver

white,
separate
from the houses,

the trees,
old woman walking
on street out front.

Eye o' the Storm

Weather's a funny
factor, like once

day breaks, storm's
lifted, or come,

faces, eyes,
like clouds drift

over this world,
are all there is

of whatever there is.

On a Theme by Lawrence, Hearing Purcell

Knowing what
knowing is,

think less
of your life as labor.

Pain's increase,
thought's random torture,

grow with intent.
Simply live.

This Day

This day after
Thanksgiving the edge
of winter
comes closer.

This grey, dulled
morning the sky
closes down on
the horizon to make

one wonder
if a life lives more
than just looking,
knowing nothing more.

Yet such a gentle
light, faded,
domestic,
impermanent—

one will not
go farther than home
to see this world
so quietly, greyly, shrunken.

The Last Mile

FOR JACK CLARKE

What's to be said
of friend dead—
eight years later?

Should he have waited
for whatever
here comes together

to make a use
for these friends and fools
must need excuse

for testament, for
interpretation,
for their own investment?

You know the world
is one *big blow*—
that's all.

I'm here as well, now
unable to say
what it is or was,

he said, more than to stay
in the body
all the way

to the grave, as it happens,
which is what scares us
then and now.

So much for the human.
No one more than any
ever did anything.

But we'll still talk about it,
as if to get out of it,
be God's little symbols . . .

At least to *stand forth* —
walk up the path,
kick the goddamn rock.

Then take deep breath
and cry —
Thank god I'm alive!

If I Had My Way

If I had my way, dear,
all these fears, these insistent
blurs of discontent would fade,

and there be
old-time meadows
with brown and white cows,

and those boulders,
still in mind, marked
the solid world. I'd

show you these ridiculous,
simple happinesses, the wonders
I've kept hold on

to steady the world—
the brook, the woods,
the paths, the clouds, the house

I lived in,
with the big barn
with my father's sign on it:

FOUR WINDS FARM.
What life ever is
stays in them.

You're young, like
they say. Your life
still comes to find

me—my honor
its choice. Here is the place
we live in

day by day, to learn
love, having it,
to begin again

again. Looking up,
this sweet room
with its colors, its forms,

has become you—
as my own life
finds its way

to you also,
wants to haul
all forward

but learns to let go,
lets the presence
of you be.

If I had my way, dear,
forever there'd be
a garden of roses—

on the old player piano
was in the sitting room
you've never seen nor will now see,

nor my mother or father,
or all that came after,
was a life lived,

all the labor, the pain?
the deaths, the wars,
the births

of my children? On
and on then—
for you and for me.

One

There are no words I know
tell where to go and how,
or how to get back again
from wherever one's been.

They don't keep directions
as tacit information.
Years of doing this and that
stay in them, yet apart.

As if words were things,
like anything. Like this one —
s i n g l e —
sees itself so.

The Fact

Think of a grand metaphor
for life's décor,
a party atmosphere
for all you love or fear —

let a daydream
make factual being,
nightmare be where
you live then.

When I'm sufficiently depressed,
I change the record,
crawl out into air,
still thankful it's there.

Elsewise the nuttiness of existence
truly confuses—
nowhere to eat
if thousands starving give you meat,

nowhere to sit
if thousands die for it,
nowhere to sleep
if thousands cannot.

Thousands, millions, billions
of people die, die,
happy or sad, starved, murdered,
or indifferent.

What's the burden then
to assume,
as 'twere load on back—
a simple fact?

Will it be right
later tonight,
when body's dumped its load
and grown silent,

when hairs grow on
in the blackness
on dead or living face,
when bones creak,

turning in bed, still alive?
What is the pattern,
the plan, makes it right
to be alive,

more than *you are,*
if dying's the onus
common to all of us?
No one gets more or less.

Can you hurry through it,
can you push and pull
all with you,
can you leave anything alone?

Do you dare to
live in the world,
this world,
equal with all —

or, thinking, remembering,
1+1=2,
that sign means one and one,
and two, are the same —

equality!
"God shed his grace on thee . . ."
How abstract
is that fucking fact.

Prayer to Hermes

FOR RAFAEL LOPEZ-PEDRAZA

Hermes, god
of crossed sticks,
crossed existence,
protect these feet

I offer. Imagination
is the wonder
of the real, and I am
sore afflicted with

the devil's doubles,
the twos, of this
half-life,
this twilight.

Neither one nor two
but a mixture
walks here
in me—

feels forward,
finds behind
the track, yet
cannot stand

still or be here
elemental, be more
or less a man,
a woman.

What I understand
of this life,
what was right
in it, what was wrong,

I have forgotten
in these days
of physical change.
I see the ways

of knowing, of
securing, life grow
ridiculous. A weakness,
a tormenting, relieving weakness

comes to me. My hand
I see at arm's end—
five fingers, fist—
is not mine?

Then must I forever
walk on, *walk on*—
as I have and
as I can?

Neither truth, nor love,
nor body itself—
nor anyone of any—
become me?

Yet questions
are tricks,
for me—
and always will be.

This moment the grey,
suffusing fog
floats in the quiet courtyard
beyond the window—

this morning grows now
to noon, and somewhere above
the sun warms the air
and wetness drips as ever

under the grey, diffusing
clouds. This weather,
this winter, comes closer.
This—*physical* sentence.

I give all
to you, hold
nothing back,
have no strength to.

My luck
is your gift,
my melodious
breath, my stumbling,

my twisted commitment,
my vagrant
drunkenness, my confused
flesh and blood.

All who know me
say, *why* this man's
persistent pain, the scarifying
openness he makes do with?

Agh! brother spirit,
what do they know
of whatever *is* the instant
cannot wait a minute—

will find heaven in hell,
will be there again even now,
and *will* tell of itself
all, *all* the world.

Mirrors

In Mirrours, there is the like
Angle of Incidence, from the Object
to the Glasse, and from the Glasse
to the Eye.

— FRANCIS BACON

One

First Rain

These retroactive small
instances of feeling

reach out for a common
ground in the wet

first rain of a faded
winter. Along the grey

iced sidewalk revealed
piles of dogshit, papers,

bits of old clothing, are
the human pledges,

call them, "We are here and
have been all the time." I

walk quickly. The wind
drives the rain, drenching

my coat, pants, blurs
my glasses, as I pass.

Memory, 1930

There are continuities in memory, but
useless, dissimilar. My sister's

recollection of what happened won't
serve me. I sit, intent, fat,

the youngest of the suddenly
disjunct family, whose father is

being then driven in an ambulance
across the lawn, in the snow, to die.

The Edge

Long over whatever edge,
backward a false distance,
here and now, sentiment—

to begin again, forfeit
in whatever sense an end,
to give up thought of it—

hanging on to the weather's edge,
hope, a sufficiency, thinking
of love's accident, this

long way come with no purpose,
face again, changing,
these hands, feet, beyond me,

coming home, an intersection,
crossing of one and many,
having all, having nothing—

Feeling thought, heart, head
generalities, all abstract—
no place for me or mine—

I take the world and lose it,
miss it, misplace it,
put it back or try to, can't

find it, fool it, even feel it.
The snow from a high sky,
grey, floats down to me softly.

This must be the edge
of being before the thought of it
blurs it, can only try to recall it.

Song

Love has no other friends
than those given it, as us,
in confusion of trust and dependence.

We want the world a wonder
and wait for it to become one
out of our simple bodies and minds.

No doubt one day it will
still all come true as people
do flock to it still until

I wonder where they'll all find room
to honor love in their own turn
before they must move on.

It's said the night comes
and ends all delusions and dreams,
in despite of our present sleeping.

But here I lie with you
and want for nothing more
than time in which to—

till love itself dies with me,
at last the end I thought to see
of everything that can be.

No! All vanity, all mind flies
but love remains, love, nor dies
even without me. Never dies.

The View

Roof pours upward,
crisscrossed with new
snow on cedar shingles
—grey-black and white—
blue over it, the
angle of looking through
window past the grape ivy
hanging from the top of it,
orange shaded light on,
place fixed by seeing
both to and from,
ignoring bricked window arch
across, just covered by
the light vertically striped
pinned to cross-rod curtain.

Human Song

What would a baby be
if we could see
him be, what would he be.

What stuff made of,
what to say to us,
that first moment.

From what has come.
Where come from—
new born babe.

What would he like,
would like us.
Would us like him.

Is he of pleasure, of pain,
of dumb indifference
or mistake made, made.

Is he alive or dead,
or unbegun, in between time
and us. Is he one of us.

Will he know us
when he's come,
will he love us.

Will we love him.
Oh tell us, tell us.
Will we love him.

Time

FOR WILLY

Out window roof's slope
of overlapped cedar shingles
drips at its edges, morning's still

overcast, grey, Sunday—
goddamn the god that will not
come to his people in their want,

serves as excuse for death—
these days, far away, blurred world
I had never believed enough.

For this wry, small, vulnerable
particular child, my son—
my dearest and only William—

I want a human world, a
chance. Is it my age
that fears, falters in some faith?

These ripples of sound, poor
useless prides of mind,
name the things, the feelings?

When I was young,
the freshness of a single
moment came to me

with all hope, all tangent wonder.
Now I am one, inexorably
in this body, in this time.

All generality? There is
no one here but words,
no thing but echoes.

Then by what imagined right
would one force another's life
to serve as one's own instance,

his significance be mine—
wanting to sing, come
only to this whining sickness . . .

Up from oneself physical
actual limit to lift
thinking to its intent

if such in world there is
now all truth to tell
this child is all it is

or ever was. The place of
time oneself in the net
hanging by hands will

finally lose their hold,
fall. Die. Let this son
live, let him live.

Self-portrait

He wants to be
a brutal old man,
an aggressive old man,
as dull, as brutal
as the emptiness around him,

He doesn't want compromise,
nor to be ever nice
to anyone. Just mean,
and final in his brutal,
his total, rejection of it all.

He tried the sweet,
the gentle, the "oh,
let's hold hands together"
and it was awful,
dull, brutally inconsequential.

Now he'll stand on
his own dwindling legs.
His arms, his skin,
shrink daily. And
he loves, but hates equally.

Greeting Card

FOR PEN

Expect the unexpected
and have a happy day . . .

Know love's surety
either in you or me.

Believe you are always
all that human is

in loyalty, in generosity,
in wise, good-natured clarity.

No one more than you
would be love's truth—

nor less
deserve ever unhappiness.

Therefore wonder's delight
will make the way.

Expect the unexpected
and have a happy day . . .

Prospect

Green's the predominant color here,
but in tones so various, and muted

by the flatness of sky and water,
the oak trunks, the undershade back of the lawns,

it seems a subtle echo of itself.
It is the color of life itself,

it used to be. Not blood red,
or sun yellow—but this green,

echoing hills, echoing meadows,
childhood summer's blowsiness, a youngness

one remembers hopefully forever.
It is thoughtful, provokes here

quiet reflections, settles the self
down to waiting now apart

from time, which is done,
this green space, faintly painful.

The Sound

Early mornings, in the light still
faint making stones, herons, marsh
grass all but indistinguishable in the muck,

one looks to the far side, of the sound, the sand
side with low growing brush and
reeds, to the long horizontal of land's edge,

where the sea is, on that
other side, that outside, place of
imagined real openness, restless, eternal ocean.

Retrospect

Thanks for
what will be
the memory
if it is.

One World

Tonight possibly they'll
invite us down to the barricades
finally sans some tacit
racism or question of our authenticity.

No one will be ashamed he
has to face the prospect
of being blown up alone in
the privacy of his own home.

One can be looted, burned,
bombed, etc., in company,
a Second World War sequel for real,
altogether, now and forever.

Money

Stand up, heart, and take it.
Boat tugs at mooring.
Just a little later, a little later.

More you wanted, more you got.
The shock of recognition, like they say,
better than digitalis.

You want that sailboat sailing by?
Reach out and take it
if you can, if you must.

You talk a lot to yourself
about what you don't want
these days, adding up figures, costs.

Here in the rented house on the water
for the proverbial two months,
it's still not enough.

You

You will remember little of yourself
as you used to be. One expects this

familiar human convenience. I want
a more abrupt person, more explicit.

Nothing you did was lost, it was
real as you were, and are. But

this present collection of *myselves*
I cannot distinguish as other than

a collection. You talk to yourself
and you get the answers expected.

But oneself is real. There is, presumably,
all that is here to prove it.

Mother's Voice

In these few years
since her death I hear
mother's voice say
under my own, I won't

want any more of that.
My cheekbones resonate
with her emphasis. Nothing
of not wanting only

but the distance there from
common fact of others
frightens me. I look out
at all this demanding world

and try to put it quietly back,
from me, say, thank you,
I've already had some
though I haven't

and would like to
but I've said no, she has,
it's not my own voice anymore.
It's higher as hers was

and accommodates too simply
its frustrations when
I at least think I want more
and must have it.

Dreams

I was supposed to wake
but didn't, slept
seeing the separate
heads and faces,

the arms, the legs,
the parts of a person
specific. As always
one was taken

to the end, the place
where the horror dawns
and one has killed
or been killed.

Then to wake up would be
no help in time.
The grey light breaks into
dawn. The day begins.

Outside

The light now meets
with the shuddering branch.
What I see
distorts the image.

This is an age
of slow determinations,
goes up the stairs
with dulled will.

Who would accept death
as an end
thinks he can
do what he wants to.

There

With all I know
remembering a page
clear to my eye
and in my mind

a single thing
of such size
it can find
no other place—

Written word
once so clear
blurred content
now loses detail.

The Visit

No resolution,
understanding
when she comes
abrupt, final

anger, rage
at the painful
displacement,
the brutal use

of rational love,
the meagerness
of the intentional
offering.

Versions

AFTER HARDY

Why would she come to him,
come to him,
in such disguise

to look again at him —
look again —
with vacant eyes —

and why the pain still,
the pain —
still useless to them —

as if to begin again —
again begin —
what had never been?

.

Why be
persistently
hurtful —
no truth
to tell
or wish to?
Why?

.

The weather's still grey
and the clouds gather
where they once walked
out together,

greeted the world with
a faint happiness,
watched it die
in the same place.

Death

Once started nothing stops
but for moment
breath's caught time
stays patient.

There Is Water

There is water
at road's end
like a shimmer,
a golden opening,

if sun's right
over trees
where the land
runs down

some hill
seeming to fall
to a farther reach
of earth but

no woods left
in the surrounding
wet air. Only the heavy
booming surf.

Age

He is thinking of everyone
he ever knew
in no order, lets
them come or go

as they will. He wonders
if he'll see them again,
if they'll remember him,
what they'll do.

There's no surprise now,
not the unexpected
as it had been. He's agreed
to being more settled.

Yet, like they say, as he
gets older, he knows
he won't expect it, not
the aches and pains.

He thinks he'll hate it
and when he does die
at last, he supposes
he still won't know it.

Box

Say it,
you're afraid

but of what
you can't locate.

You love yet
distracted fear

the body's change,
yourself inside it.

Two

Oh Love

My love is a boat
floating
on the weather, the water.

She is a stone
at the bottom of the ocean.
She is the wind in the trees.

I hold her
in my hand
and cannot lift her,

can do nothing
without her. Oh love,
like nothing else on earth!

Wind Lifts

Wind lifts lightly
the leaves, a flower,
a black bird

hops up to the bowl
to drink. The sun
brightens the leaves, back

of them darker branches,
tree's trunk. Night is still
far from us.

The Movie Run Backward

The words will one day come
back to you, birds returning,
the movie run backward.

Nothing so strange in its talk,
just words. The people
who wrote them are the dead ones.

This here paper talks like anything
but is only one thing,
"birds returning."

You can "run the movie
backward" but "the movie run
backward." The movie run backward.

Bresson's Movies

A movie of Robert
Bresson's showed a yacht,
at evening on the Seine,
all its lights on, watched

by two young, seemingly
poor people, on a bridge adjacent,
the classic boy and girl
of the story, any one

one cares to tell. So
years pass, of course, but
I identified with the young,
embittered Frenchman,

knew his almost complacent
anguish and the distance
he felt from his girl.
Yet another film

of Bresson's has the
aging Lancelot with his
awkward armor standing
in a woods, of small trees,

dazed, bleeding, both he
and his horse are,
trying to get back to
the castle, itself of

no great size. It
moved me, that
life was after all
like that. You are

in love. You stand
in the woods, with
a horse, bleeding.
The story is true.

Ambition

Couldn't guess it,
couldn't be it—

wasn't ever
there then. Won't

come back, don't
want it.

Fort Collins Remembered

To be backed
down the road
by long view

of life's imponderable
echo of time spent
car's blown motor

town on edge of
wherever fifty
bucks you're lucky.

Beyond

Whether in the world below or above,
one was to come to it,
rejected, accepted, in some

specific balance. There was to be
a reckoning, a judgment
unavoidable, and one would know

at last the fact of a life lived,
objectively, divinely, as it were,
acknowledged in whatever faith.

So that looking now for where
"an ampler aether clothes the meads with roseate light,"
or simply the "pallid plains of asphodel,"

the vagueness, the question, goes in,
discovers only emptiness — as if
the place itself had been erased,

was only forever an idea and
could never be found nor had it been.
And there was nothing ever beyond.

Stone

Be as careful, as rational,
as you will but know
nothing of such kind is true

more than fits the skin
and so covers what's within
with another soft covering

that can leave the bones alone,
that can be as it will alone,
and stays as quiet, as stable, as stone.

Elements

Sky cries down
and water looks up.

Air feels everywhere
sudden bumps, vague emptiness.

Fire burns. Earth is left
a waste, inhuman.

Still Too Young

I was talking to older
man on the phone

who's saying something
and something are five

when I think it's four,
and all I'd hoped for

is going up in abstract smoke,
and this call is from California

and selling a house,
in fact, two houses,

is losing me money more
than I can afford to,

and I thought I was winning
but I'm losing again

but I'm too old to do it again
and still too young to die.

Sad Advice

If it isn't fun, don't do it.
You'll have to do enough that isn't.

Such is life, like they say,
no one gets away without paying

and since you don't get to keep it
anyhow, who needs it.

Two Kids

Two kids, small
black sculpture. In
trepidation she turns

to him who bends
forward to, as they say,
assist her. It is,

the proposal is,
her fear provokes her,
fear of a frog

crouching at the far
end of this banal, small,
heavy hunk of metal

must have cost a
pretty penny so
to arouse in mind's

back recesses
a comfortable sense
of incest? Or else

the glass table top on which it sits
so isolates this meager action
– or else the vegetation,

the fern stalks, beside them
hang over, making privacy
a seeming thought

of these two who,
as Keats said, will never move
nor will any of it

beyond the moment,
the small minutes of some hour,
like waiting in a dentist's office.

Wishes

FOR JOHN AND DEBORA DALEY

Lunch with its divers
orders of sliced
chicken going by on

the lazy susan with
the cucumber, the goat cheese,
the remnants of the rice

salad left from last night.
All in a whirl the participants
and their very young

children eat, and
drink, and watch for
the familial move will

betoken home ground
in the heat of sultry summer
through the wall-to-wall

glass and beyond to the oaks,
the exhilarated grass, the
fall-off to the marshy

waters, the long-legged white
birds spearing fish.
Are we not well met

here, factually nowhere
ever known to us before,
and will we not forever

now remember this? One wonders,
and hopes, loves, conjectures
as to the lives of others,

all others, from other worlds
still here and always
everywhere about us, none

to be left out. No
memory, no thought,
less. Nothing forgot.

Echoes

Step through the mirror,
faint with the old desire.

Want it again,
never mind who's the friend.

Say yes to the wasted
empty places. The guesses

were as good as any.
No mistakes.

Summer

The last waltz
pale days
jesus freaks
empty hours

of sitting around
thinking and drinking
being home
in a rented house

for the summer only
while the folks are away
and we get to use it
so long as we pay.

If

If your hair was brown
and isn't now,
if your hands were strong
and now you falter,

if your eyes were sharp
and now they blur,
your step confident
and now it's careful—

you've had the world,
such as you got.
There's nothing more,
there never was.

If Happiness

If happiness were
simple joy, bird,

beast or flower
were the so-called world

here everywhere
about us,

then love were as true
as air, as water—

as sky's light, ground's
solidness, rock's hardness,

for us, in us,
of us.

Waiting

Were you counting the days
from now till then

to what end,
what to discover,

which wasn't known
over and over?

Still Dancers

Set the theme
with a cadence
of love's old
sweet song—

No harm in
the emotional
nor in remembering all
you can or want to.

Let the faint, faded music
pour forth its wonder
and bewitch whom it will,
still dancers under the moon.

The Faces

The faces with anticipated youth
look out from the current
identifications, judge or salesman,
the neighbor, the man who killed,

mattering only as the sliding world
they betoken, the time it never
mattered to accumulate, the fact that
nothing mattered but for what one

could make of it, some passing,
oblique pleasure, a pain immense
in its intensity, a sly but
insistent yearning to outwit it

all, be different, move far, far
away, avoid forever the girl
next door, whose cracked, wrinkled
smile will still persist, still know you.

To Say It

Just now at five
the light's caught the north
side of the trees next
door, the extensive

lawn to the sea's
edge where the marsh grass
seems a yellowish
green haze in late

afternoon. Above, the clouds
move over, storm's edge
passes in bunches of fluffy
soft dark-centered blobs,

all going or gone
as the wind freshens
from the land, blowing out
to sea. Now by the edge

of the window glass at the level
of the floor the grass
has become particularized
in the late light, each

edge of grass stalk
a tenacious fact of being there,
not words only, but only words,
only these words, to say it.

If, as in a bottle, the message
has been placed, if air, water
and earth try to say so with
human agency, no matter the imperfect,

useless gesture, all that is lost,
or mistaken, the arrogance
of trying to, the light comes again,
comes here, after brief darkness is still here.

Some Echo

The ground seems almost stolid
alongside the restless water,
surface now rippled by wind
echoed by the myriad tree branches—

and thought is a patient security then,
a thing in mind at best or else
some echo of physical world
it is but can know nothing of.

Three

Such Flowers

Such flowers can bloom
blurred harsh

winter days
in house so

quietly empty.
Delight in leaves

uplifting to
cold neon or gangling

out toward faint
grey window light.

Buffalo Evening

Steady, the evening fades
up the street into sunset
over the lake. Winter sits

quiet here, snow piled
by the road, the walks stamped
down or shoveled. The kids

in the time before dinner are
playing, sliding on the old ice.
The dogs are out, walking,

and it's soon inside again,
with the light gone. Time
to eat, to think of it all.

Winter

Snow lifts it
by slowing

the movement expected,
makes walking

slower, harder,
makes face ache,

eyes blur, hands fumble,
makes the day explicit,

the night quiet,
the outside more so

and the inside glow
with warmth, with people

if you're lucky, if
world's good to you,

won't so simply
kill you, freeze you.

All the Way

Dance a little,
don't worry.

There's all the way
till tomorrow

from today
and yesterday.

Simple directions, direction,
to follow.

Kid

Smaller, no recall
of not liking one's mother

given as god was
there and forever

loving learned from her
care, bemused

distraction and
much else.

Early Reading

Break heart, peace,
shy ways of holding
to the meager thing.

Little place in mind
for large, expansive counters
such as Hulme would also

seemingly deny yet afford
with bleak moon late
rising on cold night's field.

Beside Her to Lie

He'd like the edge
of her warmth here
"beside her to lie"

in trusting comfort
no longer contests
he loves and wants her.

Circles

I took the test
and I'm not depressed.

I'm inside here,
I've locked the door,

become a tentative
security system,

sensory alerts, resonant
echoes, lights, long

empty hallways. Waves
crash against the breakwater.

It's dark out there
they think until daylight

lets them off the hook
again till the phone rings,

someone passing
looks in.

On Phrase from Ginsberg's *Kaddish*

"All girls grown old . . ."
broken, worn out

men, dead
houses gone, boats sunk

jobs lost, retired
to old-folks' home.

Eat, drink,
be merry, you fink.

Worry

So careful
of anything

thought of,
so slow

to move
without it.

Coming Home

Saturday late afternoon
with evening soon coming

grey the feel of it
snow underfoot still

weather's company
despite winter's harshness

coming up the path
with the dogs barking

home is where the heart is
this small house stays put.

Be of Good Cheer

Go down obscurely,
seem to falter

as if walking into water
slowly. Be of good cheer

and go as if indifferent,
even if not.

There are those before you
they have told you.

Help Heaven

Help heaven up out
of nothing before it
so deep and soft
lovely it feels to
be here at all now.

She Is

Far from me
thinking
her long
warmth, close-

ness, how
her face lights,
changes, how
I *miss* her,

want no
more time
without
her.

Oh

Oh like a bird
falls down

out of air,
oh like a disparate

small snowflake
melts momently.

Provincetown

Could walk on water backwards
to the very place
and all around was sand
where grandma dug, bloomers up,
with her pail, for clams.

N. Truro Light — 1946

Pushing it back to
night we went

swimming in the dark
at that light

house in N. Truro
with that Bill singing,

whistling on, later stuck
his head out subway train

N.Y. window, got killed on post,
smashed, he whistled

out there in the water
Beethoven's Ninth, we

couldn't see him, only
hear him singing on.

Rachel Had Said

FOR R. G.

Rachel had said
the persons of her life
now eighty and more
had let go themselves

into the *larger* life,
let go of it, *them*
were persons personal,
let flow so, flower,

larger, more in it,
the garden, desire,
heaven's imagination
seen in being

here among us every-
where in open
wonder about them, in
pain, in pleasure, blessed.

Question

Water all around me
the front of sky ahead
sand off to the edges
light dazzle wind

way of where waves of
pleasure it can be here
am I dead or alive
in which is it.

Tell Story

Tell story
simply
as you know
how to.

This road
has ending,
hand
in hand.

Coda

Oh Max

1
Dumbass clunk plane "American
Airlines" (well-named) waits at gate

for hour while friend in Nevada's
burned to ash. The rabbi

won't be back till Sunday.
Business lumbers on

in cheapshit world of
fake commerce, *buy and sell,*

what today, what
tomorrow. Friend's dead—

out of it, won't be back
to pay phoney dues. The best

conman in country's
gone and you're left in

plane's metal tube squeezed out
of people's pockets, pennies

it's made of, *big bucks,*
nickels, dimes all the same.

You won't understand it's forever—
one time, just *one time*

you get to play,
go for broke, *forever,* like

old-time musicians,
Thelonious, Bud Powell, Bird's

horn with the chewed-through reed,
Jamaica Plain in the '40s

—Izzy Ort's, The Savoy. Hi Hat's
now gas station. It goes fast.

Scramble it, make an omelet
out of it, for the hell of it. Eat

these sad pieces. Say it's
paper you wrote the world on

and guy's got gun to your head—
go on, he says, *eat it* . . .

You can't take it back.
It's gone. Max's dead.

2
What's memory's
agency—why so much
matter. Better remember

all one can forever—
never, *never* forget.
We met in Boston,

1947, he was out of jail
and just married, lived
in sort of hotel-like

room off Washington Street,
all the lights on,
a lot of them. I never

got to know her well,
Ina, but his daughter
Rachel I can think of

now, when she was 8,
stayed with us, Placitas, wanted bicycle,
big open-faced kid, loved

Max, her father, who,
in his own fragile way,
was good to her.

In and out
of time, first Boston,
New York later—then

he showed up in N.M.,
as I was leaving, 1956,
had the rent still paid

for three weeks on
"The Rose-Covered Cottage" in Ranchos
(where sheep ambled o'er bridge)

so we stayed,
worked the street, like they say,
lived on nothing.

Fast flashes—the women
who love him, Rena, Joyce,
Max, the *mensch,* makes

poverty almost fun,
hangs on edge, keeps traveling.
Israel—they catch him,

he told me, lifting
a bottle of scotch at the airport,
tch, tch, let him stay

(I now think) 'cause
he wants to.
Lives on kibbutz.

So back to New Mexico,
goyims' Israel sans the plan
save Max's ("Kansas City," "Terre Haute")

New Buffalo (friend told me
he yesterday saw that on bus placard
and thought, that's it! Max's place).

People and people and people.
Buddy, Wuzza, Si
Perkoff, and Sascha,

Big John C., and Elaine,
the kids. Joel and Gil,
LeRoi, Cubby, back and back

to the curious end
where it bends away into
nowhere or Christmas he's

in the army, has come home,
and father, in old South Station,
turns him in as deserter, ashamed,

ashamed of his son. Or the man
Max then kid with his papers
met nightly at Summer Street

subway entrance and on Xmas
he gives him a dime for a tip . . .
No, old man, your son

was not wrong. "America"
just a vagueness, another place,
works for nothing, gets along.

3
In air
there's nowhere
enough not
here, nothing

left to speak
to but you'll
know as plane
begins its

descent, like
they say, it
was the place
where you were,

Santa Fe
(holy fire) with
mountains
of blood.

4

Can't leave, never could,
without more, just
one more

for the road.
Time to go makes
me stay —

Max, *be happy,*
be good, broken
brother, *my man,* useless

words
now
forever.

> — *for Max Finstein died circa 11:00 a.m.*
> *driving truck (Harvey Mudd's) to*
> *California — near Las Vegas — 3/17/82.*

Memory Gardens

Well, while I'm here I'll
       do the work —
and what's the Work?
      To ease the pain of living.
Everything else, drunken
          dumbshow.

  — ALLEN GINSBERG,
   "MEMORY GARDENS"

One

Heaven Knows

Seemingly never until one's dead
is there possible measure—

but of what then or for what
other than the same plagues

attended the living with misunderstanding
and wanted a compromise as pledge

one could care for any of them
heaven knows, if that's where one goes.

Forty

The forthright, good-natured faith
of man hung on crane up

forty stories with roof scaffolding
burning below him forty feet,

good warm face, black hair,
confidence. He said, when

the firemen appeared, he said
I'm glad to see you,

glad not to be there alone.
How old? Thirty, thirty-five?

He has friends to believe in,
those who love him.

Out

Within pitiless
indifference
things left
out.

New England

Work, Christian, work!
Love's labors before you go
carrying lights like the
stars are all out and
tonight is the night.

Too Late

You tried to answer the questions attractively,
your name, your particular interests,

what you hoped life would prove,
what you owned and had with you,

your so-called billfold an umbilical,
useless, to the sack you'd carried

all your sad life, all your vulnerability,
but couldn't hide, couldn't now say,

brown hair, brown eyes, steady,
I think I love you.

Room

Quick stutters of incidental
passage going back

and forth, quick
breaks of pattern, slices

of the meat, two
rotten tomatoes, an incidental

snowstorm, death, a girl
that looks like you later

than these leaves of
grass, trees, birds, under

water, empty passage-
way, and no way back.

Hotel

It isn't in the world of
fragile relationships

or memories, nothing
you could have brought with you.

It's snowing in Toronto.
It's four-thirty, a winter evening,

and the tv looks like a faded
hailstorm. The people

you know are down the hall,
maybe, but you're tired,

you're alone, and that's happy.
Give up and lie down.

Echo

Pushing out from
this insistent

time makes
all of it

empty, again
memory.

Earth

And as the world is flat or round
out over those difficult dispositions

of actual water, actual earth,
each thing invariable, specific,

I think no rock's hardness,
call on none to gainsay me,

be only here as and forever
each and every thing is.

Dogs

I've trained them
to come,

to go away again,
to sit, to stand,

to wait
on command,

or I'd like to
be the master who

tells them all
they can't do.

Vision

Think of the size of it,
so big, if you could remember
what it was or where.

Religion

Gods one would have
hauled out like props
to shore up the invented
inside-out proposals

of worlds equally like shams
back of a shabby curtain
only let in the duped,
the dumbly despairing.

So flutter the dead
back of the scene
and along with them
the possibly still living.

The Rock

Shaking hands again
from place of age,
out to the one

is walking down
the garden path
to be as all reunited.

Thanksgiving's Done

All leaves gone, yellow
light with low sun,

branches edged
in sharpened outline

against far-up pale sky.
Nights with their blackness

and myriad stars, colder
now as these days go by.

Go

Push that little
thing up and the
other right down.
It'll work.

Main and Merrimac

"It just plain
hurts to work—"
Christ holds
up hands in
mock despair
concrete bright
sun with faint
first green of
leaves this morn-
ing's gone to
spring's first day.

For Pen

Lady moon
light white
flowers open
in sweet silence.

For J. D.

Seeing is believing —
times such things
alter all one
had known.

These times, places,
old, echoing
clothes, hands — tools,
almost walking.

Your heart *as big as all outdoors* . . .
where tree grows,
gate was
waiting.

Always

Sweet sister Mary's gone
away. Time fades on and on.

The morning was so bright, so clear
blurs in the eye, fades also.

Time tells what after all.
It's always now, always here.

Edge

Edge of place
put on between

its proposed
place in

time
and space.

Massachusetts May

Month one was born in
particular emphasis
as year comes round
again. Laconic, diverse

sweet May of my boyhood,
as the Memorial Day Parade
marches through those memories.
Or else the hum and laze

of summer's sweet patterns,
dragonflies, grasshoppers,
ladyslippers, and ponds—
School's end. Summer's song.

Memories

Hello, duck,
in yellow

cloth stuffed from
inside out,

little
pillow.

Echo

Back in time
for supper
when the lights

Two

Wall

I've looked at this wall
for months, bricks
faded, chipped, edge of roof

fixed with icicles
like teeth,
arch of window

opposite, blistered
white paint, a trim
of grey blue.

Specific limit—
of what? A shell
of house, no one's home,

tenuous,
damp emptiness
under a leaky roof.

Careless of what else,
wall so close,
insistent,

to my own—
can push
with eye, thinking

where one can't go,
those crushed
in so-called blackness,

despair. This easy
admission's
no place walls

can echo,
real or unreal.
They sit between

inside and out—
like in school, years ago,
we saw *Wall,* heard

Wall say, "Thus have I,
Wall, my part discharged so;/
And, being done,

thus Wall away doth go"—
Clouds overhead, patch of
shifting blue sky. Faint sun.

I'll Win

I'll win the way
I always do
by being gone
when they come.

When they look, they'll see
nothing of me
and where I am
they'll not know.

This, I thought, is my way
and right or wrong
it's me. Being dead, then,
I'll have won completely.

Eats

Self-shrinking focus
mode of deployment
of people met in casual
engagement, social—

Not the man I am
or even was, have constructed
some pattern, place
will be as all.

Bored, shrink into
isolated fading
out of gross, comfortable
contact, hence *out to lunch*.

For the New Year

Rid forever of *them* and *me*,
the ridiculous small places
of the patient hates, the meager

agreement of unequal people—
at last all subject to
hunger, despair, a common grief.

Bookcase

One cannot offer
to emptiness

more than regret. The persons
no longer are there,

their presence become
a resonance, something

inside. Postcard—
"still more to have . . .

"of talking to you"—
found in book

in this chaos—
dead five years.

Baby Disaster

Blurred headlights of the cars out there
war of the worlds or something,
ideas of it all like dropped change,
trying to find it on the sidewalk at night.

Nothing doing anymore, grown up, moved out,
piddling little's going to come of it,
all you put in the bank or spent
you didn't want to, wanted to keep it all.

Walk on by, baby disaster.
Sad for us all finally, totally,
going down like in Sargasso Sea
of everything we ever thought to.

Sound

Shuddering racket of
air conditioner's colder

than imagined winter,
standing lonely,

constancy's not
only love's,

not such faith
in mere faithfulness—

sullen sound.

For J. D. (2)

Pass on by, love,
wait by that garden gate.
Swing on, up
on heaven's gate.

The confounding, confronted
pictures of world
brought to signs
of its insistent self

are here in all colors, sizes—
a heart as big as all outdoors,
a weather of spaces,
intervals between silences.

Picture

FOR D. L.

Great giggles,
chunky lumps,
packed flesh,
good nature—

like an apple,
a pear, an immaculate
strawberry, a
particular pomegranate.

And that's the way you saw me, love?
Just so.
Was there nothing else struck you?
No.

Four for John Daley

MOTHER'S THINGS
I wanted approval,
carrying with me
things of my mother's
beyond their use to me—

worn-out clock,
her small green lock box,
father's engraved brass plate
for printing calling cards—

such size of her still
calls out to me
with that silently
expressive will.

ECHO
Lonely in
no one
to hold it with—

the responsible
caring
for those one's known.

LEAVING
My eye teared,
lump in throat—
I was going
away from here

and everything that
had come with me
first was waiting
again to be taken.

All the times
I'd looked, held,
handled that or this
reminded me

no fairness, justice,
in life, not
that can stand
with those abandoned.

BUFFALO AFTERNOON
Greyed board fence
past brown open door,
overhead weather's
early summer's.

The chairs sit various,
what's left, the
emptiness, this
curious waiting to go.

I look up to eyes
of Willy's battered
plastic horse, a dog
for its face.

All here,
even in the absence
as if all were
so placed in vacant space.

Fort William Henry/Pemaquid

Squat round stone tower
o'erlooks the quiet water.

Might in olden days here
had literally accomplished power

as they must have hauled the rocks
from the coves adjacent

to defend their rights
in this abstract place

of mind and far waters
they'd come all the way over

to where presently small son paddles,
flops on bottom in sea's puddle.

Nothing

Ant pushes across rock face.
No sign of age there

nor in the outstretched water
looks like forever.

Dried seaweed, this ground-down sand,
or the sky where sun's reached peak

and day moves to end—
still nothing done, enough said.

For Ted Berrigan

After, size of place
you'd filled
in suddenly emptied
world all too apparent

and as if New England
shrank, grew physically
smaller like Connecticut,
Vermont—all the little

things otherwise unattended
so made real by you,
things to do today,
left empty, waiting

sadly for no one
will come again now.
It's all moved inside,
all that dear world

in mind for forever,
as long as one walks
and talks here,
thinking of you.

Hotel Schrieder, Heidelberg

Offed tv screen's
reflection room
across with gauze
draped window see
silent weeping face
Marcel Marceau from
balcony seat was memory's
Paris early fifties how
was where and when
with whom we
sat there, watching?

"Ich Bin . . ."

Ich Bin
2 *Öl*-tank

yellow squat
by railroad

shed train's
zapped past

round peculiar
empty small

town's ownership
fields' flat

production towered
by obsolescent hill-

side memory echoing
old worn-out castle.

Après Anders

HAHA
In her hair the
moon, with
the moon, wakes water—

balloon hauls her
into the blue. She

fängt, she
in the woods
faints, finds, fakes

fire, high in
Erlen, oil, Earl—

like a *Luftschiffern*,
tails of high clouds up
there, one says.

KAPUT KASPER'S LATE LOVE
I was
"kaput Kasper"
in *Fensterfrost,*

window shade auntie,
mother's faltering bundle.
Blood flecks on some
wind flint horizon.

I knew my swollen loaf,
Lauf, like, out, *aus*
es floats, it *flötete.*

Sie sagte, said
the night stuck
two eyes in her heart (head).

I *griff,* grabbed, griped,
in the empty holes, held
on to holes

unter der Stirn,
under stars, the stars
in the sky tonight.

DEN ALTEN
Then to old Uncle Emil
den du immer mimst
you always

missed,
missed most,
häng einem alten Haus

in fear, hung
from a rafter, a
beam old

Uncle Emil you
immer mimst
over the logical river

Fluss in the
truly really
feuchten clay, fucked finished clay.

LATE LOVE
Stuck in her stone hut
he fights to get the window up.

Her loopy Dachshunds
have made off with the pupils

of his eyes, like, or else
now from summit to summit

of whatever mountains against which
he thinks he hears the stars crash,

sounds truly *nada*
in all the sad façade.

AGAIN
The woman who
came out of the shadow

of the trees asked
after a time "what time is it"

her face
for a second

in my head
was there again

and I felt again
as against this emptiness

where also
I'd been.

Waiting

Waiting for the object,
the abject adjunct—

the loss of feel here,
field, faded.

Singing inside,
outside grey, wet,

cold out. The weather
doesn't know it,

goes only on to
wherever.

Hands

Reaching out to shake,
take, the hand,

hands, take in
hand hands.

Three

". . . come, poppy, when will you bloom?"

    – CHARLES OLSON

Fathers

Scattered, aslant
faded faces a column
a rise of the packed
peculiar place to a
modest height makes
a view of common lots
in winter then, a ground
of battered snow crusted
at the edges under
it all, there under
my fathers their
faded women, friends,
the family all echoed,
names trees more tangible
physical place more tangible
the air of this place the road
going past to Watertown
or down to my mother's
grave, my father's grave, not
now this resonance of
each other one was his, his
survival only, his curious
reticence, his dead state,
his emptiness, his acerbic
edge cuts the hands to
hold him, hold on, wants
the ground, *wants* this frozen ground.

Memory Gardens

Had gone up to
down or across dis-
placed eagerly
unwitting hoped for

mother's place in time
for supper just
to say anything
to her again one

simple clarity her
unstuck glued
deadness emptied
into vagueness hair

remembered wisp that
smile like half
her eyes brown eyes
her thinning arms

could lift her
in my arms so
hold to her so
take her in my arms.

Flicker

In this life the
half moment
ago is just

at this edge
of curious place you
reach for feel

that instant shining
even still wet's
gone faded flashlight.

My Own Stuff

"My own stuff" a
flotsam I could
neither touch quite
nor get hold of, fluff,
as with feathers, milk-
weed, the evasive
lightness distracted yet
insistent to touch
it kept poking, trying
with my stiffened
fingers to get hold of
its substance I had
even made to be
there its only
reality my own.

Window

The upper part is snow,
white, lower, grey
to brown, a thicket,
lacing, light seeming
hedge of branches, twigs,
growths of a tree, trees,
see eyes, holes, through
the interlacings, the white
emphatic spaced places
of the snow, the gravity,
weight, holds it, on top,
as down under, the grey,
brown, edged red, or
ground it has to come to,
must all come down.

Winter Morning

The sky's like a pewter
of curiously dulled blue,
and "My heart's in the highlands . . . ,"
feels the day beginning again.

And whatever, whatever, says it
again, and stays here, stays
here with its old hands,
holds on with its stiff, old fingers,

can come too, like they say,
can come with me into this patient weather,
and won't be left alone, no, never alone ever again,
in whatever time's left for us here.

Questions

In the photograph you felt
grey, disregarded, your head
obscured by the company
around you, presuming
some awkward question. Were you dead?

Could this self-indulgence extend
to all these others, even
persuade them to do something
about you, or *with* you, given
they had their own things to do?

Lovers

Remember? as kids
we'd looked in crypt
had we fucked? we
walked a Saturday
in cemetery it
was free the flowers
the lanes we looked
in past the small
barred window into
dark of tomb when
it looked out at us
face we saw white
looking out at us
inside the small
room was it man
who worked there? dead
person's fraught skull?

Funeral

Why was grandma
stacked in sitting room
so's people could come
in, tramp through.

What did we eat
that day before
we all drove off
to the cemetery in Natick

to bury her with grandpa
back where the small air-
port plane flew over
their modest lot there

where us kids could
look through the bushes,
see plane flying around or
sitting on the ground.

Supper

Time's more than
twilight mother at
the kitchen table over
meal the boiled potatoes
Theresa's cooked with meat.

Classical

One sits vague in this sullenness.
Faint, greying winter, hill
with its agéd, incremental institution,
all a seeming dullness of enclosure

above the flat lake—oh youth,
oh cardboard cheerios of time,
oh helpless, hopeless faith of empty trust,
apostrophes of leaden aptitude, my simple children,

why not anger, an argument, a proposal,
why the use simply of all you are or might be
by whatever comes along, your persons
fixed, hung, splayed carcasses, on abstract rack?

One instant everything must always change,
your life or death, your articulate fingers lost
in meat time, head overloaded, fused circuit,
all cheap tears, regrets, permissions forever utterly forgot.

Mother's Photograph

Could you see present
sad investment of
person, its clothes,
gloves and hat,

as against yourself
backed to huge pine tree,
lunch box in hand in
homemade dress aged

ten, to go to school
and learn to be somebody,
find the way will
get you out of the

small place of home
and bring them with
you, out of it too,
sit them down in a new house.

Valentine

Had you a dress
would cover you all
in beautiful echoes
of all the flowers I know,

could you come back again,
bones and all,
just to talk
in whatever sound,

like letters spelling words,
this one says, *Mother,
I love you* —
that one, *my son.*

Lecture

What was to talk to,
around in half-circle,
the tiers, ledges
of their persons

attending expectation,
something's to happen,
waiting for words,
explanations—

thought of cigarette
smoke, a puff recollected,
father's odor
in bed years ago.

Back

Suppose it all turns into, again,
just the common, the expected
people, and places, the distance
only some change and possibly one

or two among them all, gone—
that word again—or simply more
alone than either had been
when you'd first met them. But you

also are not the same,
as if whatever you were were
the memory only, your hair, say,
a style otherwise, eyes now

with glasses, clothes even
a few years can make look
out of place, or where you
live now, the phone, all of it

changed. Do you simply give
them your address? Who?
What's the face in the mirror then.
Who are you calling.

Knock Knock

Say nothing
to it.
Push it away.
Don't answer.

Be grey,
oblique presence.
Be nothing
there.

If it speaks
to you, it
only wants
you for itself

and it has
more than you,
much
more.

Heavy

Friend's story of dead whale on California beach
which the people blow up to get rid of and for weeks
after they're wiping the putrescent meat off their feet,

like, and if that's a heavy one, consider Meese
and what it takes to get rid of mice
and lice and just the nice people next door, *oh yeah . . .*

Skin and Bones

It ain't no sin
to sit down
take off your coat
wait for whatever

happens here
whenever it happens
for whatever.
It's your own skin.

The Doctor

Face of my
father looks out

from magazine's
page on back

of horse at eight
already four

more than
I was when

the doctor died
as both

mother and Theresa
used to say, "the

doctor," whose
saddened son I

was and have
to be, my sister

older speaks of
him, "He felt

that with Bob
he was starting

over, perhaps, and
resolved not

to lose this son
as he had Tom and Phil . . ."

Nothing said
to me, no words more

than echoes, a
smell I remember

of cigarette box, a
highball glass,

man in bed with
mother, the voice

lost now. "Your
father was such

a Christmas fellow!"
So happy, empty

in the leftover
remnants of whatever

it was, the doctor's
house, the doctor's family.

Lost

One could reach up into
the air, to see if it was

still there, shoved back
through the hole, the little

purpose, hidden it was,
the small, persisting agencies,

arms and legs, the ears
of wonder covered with area,

all eyes, the echoes, the aches
and pains of patience, the

inimitable here and now of all,
ever again to be one and only one,

to look back to see the long distance
or to go forward, having only lost.

Old

Its fears are
particular, head,

hands, feet, the
toes in two

patient rows,
and what comes

now is less,
least of all it

knows, wants in
any way to know.

There

On such a day
did it happen

by happy coincidence
just here.

Language

Are all your
preoccupations un-

civil, insistent
caviling, mis-

taken dis-
criminating?

Days

FOR H. H. C.

In that strange light,
garish like wet blood,

I had no expectations
or hopes, nothing any more

one shouts at life to wake it up,
be nice to us — simply scared

you'd be hurt, were already
changed. I was, your head

out, looked —   I want each
day for you, each single day

for you, give them
as I can to you.

Heavenly Hannah

Oh Hannie
help me
help

Four

A Calendar

THE DOOR
Hard to begin
always again and again,

open that door
on yet another year

faces two ways
but goes only one.

Promises, promises . . .
What stays true to us

or to the other
here waits for us.

(January)

HEARTS
No end to it if
"heart to heart"
is all there is

to buffer, put against
harshness of this weather,
small month's meagerness—

"Hearts are trumps,"
win out again
against all odds,

beat this
drab season of bitter cold
to save a world.

(February)

MARCH MOON
Already night and day move
more closely, shyly, under this frozen

white cover, still rigid with
locked, fixed, deadened containment.

The dog lies snuffling, snarling
at the sounds beyond the door.

She hears the night, the new moon,
the white, wan stars, the

emptiness momently will break
itself open, howling, intemperate.

(March)

"WHAN THAT APRILLE . . ."
"When April with his showers sweet
the drought of March has pierced to the root
and bathed every vein in such liqueur
its virtue thus becomes the flower . . ."

When faded harshness moves to be
gone with such bleakness days had been,
sunk under snows had covered them,
week after week no sun to see,

then restlessness resolves in rain
after rain comes now to wash all clean
and soften buds begin to spring
from battered branches, patient earth.

Then into all comes life again,
which times before had one thought dead,
and all is outside, nothing in—
and so it once more does begin.

(April)

WYATT'S MAY

In May my welth and eke my liff, I say,
have stonde so oft in such perplexitie . . .
— SIR THOS. WYATT

In England May's mercy
is generous. The mustard

covers fields in broad swaths,
the hedges are white flowered—

but it is meager, so said.
Having tea here, by the river,

huge castle, cathedral, time
passes by in undigested,

fond lumps. Wyatt died
while visiting friends nearby,

and is buried in Sherborne Abbey
"England's first sonnet-maker . . ."

May May reward him and all
he stood for more happily now

because he sang May,
maybe for all of us:

"Arise, I say, do May some obseruance!
Let me in bed lie dreming in mischaunce . . ."

So does May's mind remember all
it thought of once.

                    (May)

SUMMER NIGHTS
Up over the edge of
the hill climbs the
bloody moon and

now it lifts the far
river to its old familiar
tune and the hazy

dreamlike field – and all
is summer quiet, summer
nights' light airy shadow.

                    (June)

"BY THE RUDE BRIDGE . . ."
Crazy wheel of days
in the heat, the revolution
spaced to summer's

insistence. That sweat,
the dust, time earlier they
must have walked, run,

all the way from Lexington
to Concord: "By the rude
bridge that arched the flood . . ."

By that enfolding small river
wanders along by grasses'
marge, by thoughtless stones.

(July)

VACATION'S END
Opened door chinks
let sun's restlessness

inside eighth month
going down now

earlier as day begins
later, time running down,

air shifts to edge
of summer's end

and here they've gone,
beach emptying

to birds, clouds,
flash of fish, tidal

waters waiting, shifting,
ripple in slight wind.

(August)

HELEN'S HOUSE
Early morning far trees lift
through mist in faint outline

under sun's first rose,
dawn's opalescence here,

fall's fading rush to color,
chill under the soft air.

Foreground's the planted small fruit trees,
cut lawn, the firs, as now

on tall dying tree beyond
bird suddenly sits on sticklike branch.

Walk off into this weather?
Meld finally in such air?

See goldenrod, marigold, yarrow, tansy
wait for their turn.

(September)

OLD DAYS
River's old look
from summers ago
we'd come to swim

now yellow, yellow
rustling, flickering
leaves in sun

middle of October
water's up, high sky's blue,
bank's mud's moved,

edge is
closer,
nearer than then.

(October)

THE TALLY
Sitting at table
wedged back against wall,

the food goes down in
lumps swallowed

in hunger, in
peculiar friendship

meets rightly again
without reason

more than common bond, the children
or the old cannot reach

for more
for themselves.

We'll wonder,
wander, in November,

count days and ways
to remember, keep away

from the tally,
the accounting.

(November)

MEMORY
I'd wanted
ease of year,
light in the darkness,
end of fears.

For the babe newborn
was my belief,
in the manger,
in that simple barn.

So since childhood
animals
brought back kindness,
made possible care.

But this world now
with its want, its pain,
its tyrannic confusions
and hopelessness,

sees no star
far shining,
no wonder as light
in the night.

Only us then
remember, discover,
still can care for
the human.

(December)

Windows

One

Song

What's in the body you've forgotten
and that you've left alone
and that you don't want—

or what's in the body that you want
and would die for—
and think it's all of it—

if life's a form to be forgotten
once you've gone and no regrets,
no one left in what you were—

That empty place is all there is,
and/if the face's remembered,
or dog barks, cat's to be fed.

I Would Have Known You Anywhere

Back of the head, hand, the hair
no longer there, blown, the impotence
of face, the place no longer there, known
you were going to be there—

You were a character of dream,
a mirror looking out, a way
of seeing into space, an
impotent emptiness I share—

This day we spoke as number,
week, or time, this place an
absent ground, a house remembered
then no place. It's gone, it's gone.

What is it sees through, becomes
reflection, empty signal of the past,
a piece I kept in mind because
I thought it had come true?

I would have known you anywhere,
brother, known we were going to meet
wherever, in the street, this echo
too. I would have known you.

The Terribly Strange Bed

I recall there being
portraits on the wall
with stiff, painted eyes
rolled round in the dark

on the wall across
from my bed and the other
in the room upstairs
where we all slept

as those eyes kept looking
the persons behind
about to kill me
only in sleep safe.

Stairway to Heaven

Point of hill
we'd come to, small
rise there, the friends
now separate, cars
back of us by
lane, the stones,
Bowditch, etc., location,
Tulip Path, hard
to find on the
shaft, that insistent
rise to heaven
goes down and down,
with names like floors,
ledges of these echoes,
Charlotte, Sarah,
Thomas, Annie
and all, as with
wave of hand I'd
wanted them one
way or other to
come, go with them.

Interior

The room next to
this one with the lowered
lights, the kids watching
television, dogs squatted
on floor, and couch's

disarray, and all that
comes of living anywhere
before the next house, town,
people get to know you if
you let them, nowhere safe.

Common

Common's profound bottom
of flotsam, specious increase
of the space, a ground abounds,
a place to make it.

Not Much

Not much you ever
said you were thinking
of, not much to
say in answer.

Epic

Wanting to tell
a story,
like hell's simple invention, or
some neat recovery

of the state of grace,
I can recall lace curtains,
people I think I remember,
Mrs. Curley's face.

The World

The world so sweet its
saccharine outshot by
simple cold so colors
all against the so-called
starkness of the winter's
white and grey the
clouds the ice the
weather stables all in
flat particular light
each sunlit place so placed.

After Pasternak

Think that it's all one?
Snow's thud, the car's
stuck door, the brilliant,
patient sun—

How many millions of years
has it been coming
to be here just this once—
never returning—

Oh dull edge of prospect—
weary window on the past—
whatever is here now
cannot last.

Tree

FOR WARREN

You tree
of company—

here
shadowed branches,

small,
twisted comfortably

your size,
reddish buds' clusters—

all of
you I love

here
by the simple river.

Broad Bay

Water's a shimmer,
banks green verge,
trees' standing shadowed,
sun's light slants,
gulls settle white
on far river's length.
All is in a windy echo,
time again
    a far sense.

Just in Time

FOR ANNE

Over the unwritten
and under the written
and under and over
and in back and in front of
or up or down or in
or in place of, of not,
of this and this, of
all that is, of it.

Nationalgalerie Berlin

Nationalgalerie's
minute spasm's
self-reflective —
art's meager agony?

Two hundred years
zap past
in moment's
echoing blast!

No one apparently left
to say "hello" —
but for the genial
late Romanticists.

God, what a life!
All you see is *pain*.
I can't go through *that* again
— gotta go!

.

Trying to get *image of man*
like trying on suit,
too small, too loose,
too late, too soon—

Wrong fit. Wrong time.

And you look out of
your tired head,
still stark naked,
and you go to bed.

    .

"Bellevue-Tower"
could be Brooklyn,
The roller skaters
go round and around on the plaza,

like "In Brueghel's great picture, The Kermess . . ."
Their rhythmic beauty
is so human, so human.
I watch and watch.

    .

Kids now with skateboards.
Edge of their chatter,
boys, voices changing,
lower, grow harsher.

This is the life of man,
the plans, the ways
you have to do it.
"Practice makes perfect."

    .

BY THE CANAL / SITTING
The rippled, shelved
surface of water,
quiet canal, the chunky
horse chestnut trees spread over
reflected in edge of darker
surface where else the light
shows in endless small rows
of slight, securing peace and quiet.

Further off, on each side,
cars, buses, trucks, bikes, and people.

But man and boy
pass back of me, spin of wheels,
murmur of their voices.

Life

FOR BASIL

Specific, intensive clarity,
like nothing else
is anything
but itself—

so echoes all,
seen, felt, heard
or tasted, the one
and many. But

my slammed fist
on door, asking
meager, repentant entry
wants more.

Dialing for Dollars

CHOO CHOO
My mother just on edge
of unexpected death the
fact of one operation over
successful says, *it's all
free, Bob! You don't
have to pay for any of it!*
Life, like. Waiting for the train.

.

LIKE MINE
I'll always love
you no matter you
get all that money
and don't need a
helping hand like mine.

.

WAITING
I've never had the
habit of money but
have at times wanted
it, enough to give
myself and friends an
easy time over the
hump but you can
probably keep it, I'm
just here breathing, brother,
not exactly beside you.

.

THE WILLYS
Little
dollar
bills.

Picture

The scale's wrong. Kid's
leaned up against
Dad's huge leg, a

tree trunk, unfeeling bark,
rushing waters
of piss? Must be it

smells like toast,
like granular egg
or all night coffee

on all alone. All
so small,
so far to go.

Leaving

Where to go
if into blank wall
and back of you
you can't get to—

So night is black
and day light,
ground, water
elemental.

It all accumulates
a place, something real
in place.
There it is—

till it's time to go,
like they say,
but the others
want to stay, and will.

Nature Morte

It's still
life. It
just ain't moving.

Fleurs

Clumped Clares.
Asphobellies.
Blumenschein.

The Company

FOR THE SIGNET SOCIETY, APRIL 11, 1985

Backward—as if retentive.
"The child is father to the man"
or some such echo of device,
a parallel of use and circumstance.

Scale become implication.
Place, postcard determinant—
only because someone sent it.
Relations—best if convenient.

"Out of all this emptiness
something must come . . ." Concomitant
with the insistent banality, small, still
face in mirror looks simply vacant.

Hence blather, disjunct, incessant
indecision, moving along on
road to next town where what waited
was great expectations again, empty plate.

So there they were, expectably ambivalent,
given the Second World War
"to one who has been long in city pent,"
trying to make sense of it.

We—*morituri*—blasted from classic
humanistic *noblesse oblige,* all the garbage
of either so-called side, hung on
to what we thought we had, an existential

raison d'être like a pea
some faded princess tries to sleep on,
and when that was expectably soon gone,
we left. We walked away.

Recorders ages hence will look for us
not only in books, one hopes, nor only under rocks
but in some common places of feeling,
small enough — but isn't the human

just that echoing, resonant edge
of what it knows it knows,
takes heart in remembering
only the good times, yet

can't forget whatever it was,
comes here again, fearing this
is the last day, this is the last,
the last, the last.

Two
WINDOW

Scales

FOR BUDDY

Such small dimension
finally, the comfortable
end of it, the people
fading, world shrunk

to some recollected
edge of where it used to be,
and all around a sound
of coming, going, rustle

of neighboring movement out there
where as ever what one finally
sees, hears, wants, waits
still to recognize — is it

the sun? Grass, ground,
dog's bark, bird, the
opening, high clouds, fresh,
lifting day — *someone?*

Xmas

I'm sure there's a world I
can get to by walking another
block in the direction that
was pointed out to me by any-

one I was with and would even
talk to me that late at
night and with everything
confused—I know—the

kids tired, nerves stretched—
and all, and this person, old
man, Santa Claus! by
god—the reindeer, the presents.

Window

THEN
The window had
been half
opened and the

door also
opened, and the
world then

invited, waited,
and one
entered

.

X
The world is
many, the

mind is
one.

 .

WHERE
The window
opened,

beyond edge
of white hall,

light faint
shifts from back

a picture?
slurlike "wing"?

Who's
home?

 .

The roof's
above, old

reddish dulled
tiles, small

dormered windows, two
chimneys, above

the greyish,
close sky.

 .

Who's there,
old
question, who's
here.

    .

LIGHT
Light's on
now

in three
sided balcony

window mid-
building, a floor

up from street.
Wait.

Watch it.
What light

on drab earth,
place on earth—

Continue?
Where to go so

far away
from here?

Friends?
Forgotten?

Movement?
A hand just

flesh, fingers?
White—

Who threads fantastic tapestry
just for me, for me?

  •

WAITING
One could sit
minutes, hours,

days, weeks,
months, years—

all of its
rehearsal one

after one, be done
at last with it?

  •

Or could go
in

to it, be
inside

head, look
at day

turn to dark,
get rid

of it at last, think
out

of patience, give
it up?

.

Man
with paper, white,

in hand
"tells the truth"

silent, moves
past the window

away —
sits down?

Comes back,
leans

forward at waist,

somewhat stiffly —
not

old,
young, young.

.

He must love someone
and this must be the story

of how he wanted
everything rightly done

but without the provision
planned, fell forward

into it all,
could not withstand

the adamant simplicity
of life's "lifelike" reality —

even in a mirror
replaced by another —

and couldn't wait
any longer,

must have
moved here.

To "live a life" alone?
to "come home"?

To be "lost and found"
again, "never more to roam"

again. Or something more like
"the fading light," like

they say, never quite
come. Never just one.

Place

Your face
in mind, *slow* love,

slow growing, *slow*
to learn enough.

Patience to learn
to be *here,* to savor

whatever there is
out there, without you

here, here
by myself.

New World

Edenic land, Adamic person—
Foolishness is the price you'll have to pay
for such useless wisdom.

Ho Ho

FOR JOEL

I have broken
the small bounds
of this existence and
am travelling south

on route 90. It
is approximately
midnight, surrogate
earth time, and you

who could, can, and
will never take anything
seriously will die
as dumb as ever

while I alone in
state celestial shoot
forward at designed rate,
speed at last unimpeded.

Three

Seven: A Suite for Robert Therrien

STRAIGHT
They were going up in
a straight line right
to God, once they died—

The hills of home here
are a yellow pointer, again
God's simplistic finger—

Over the hill, the steeple
still glows in the late light—
all else whited out.

     .

PLATE
All I ever wanted was
a place

up there
by myself.

     .

"and the sky above—an old

blue

place" an

old

blue plate an old

blue face

.

Very carefully I
cut out an absolute

circle of blue
sky

or water. They
couldn't tell

the difference.

.

Blue plate

special

.

RED
When it goes
that fast

you don't see anything
but speed, you see

red.

.

I got something stuck
in my hand.

It was a splinter.

.

In the first World War
they had bombs

that looked like this.

    .

How fast
do you think it's going?

    .

SNOWMAN
Help the holes
be bigger. Put

your hand
in.

    .

He grew a
point on

top
of his head —

two
of them.

    .

That ice
cream cone'll

drip?

    .

Curious
key hole.

    .

I want to go into the immense
blue yonder

and I've built a negative number
times three.

.

WINGS
Those are hills out there
or mounds

Or breasts filling
the horizon.

.

It's a bird! Such
grace.

.

Sitting here
in Maine

I put you on the window sill
against the blue, white

yellow sky. You're a
sea gull suddenly.

What else
do I want.

.

Miles away they
are waiting for the promised

land again and the wind
has moved

the sand
into these shapes.

.

BOX
What do you think
he's got it for

unless
he means to use it.

.

No way
that could fit

(me)

.

"The worms
crawl in. The"

.

People walked
through the town carrying

coffins!

.

a *coffin*
fit . . .

Heh,
heh.

.

Just stand him up
in the corner.

.

BOAT
Rock me, boat.
Open, open.

Hold me,
little cupped hand.

Let me come in,
come on

board you, sail
off, *sail off* . . .

H's

Have Hannah's happy health —
have whatever, be

here, hombre . . . Her
hands upon edge

of table, her eyes
as dark centers, her

two teeth—but all,
her climbing, sacklike,

limp, her hands out-
stretched, or simply out

to it, her coming here,
her, all of her, her

words of her, *Hannah,
Hannie,* Good girl,

good. So we go
on with it. So is

Hannah
in this world.

After Frost

FOR SHERMAN PAUL

He comes here
by whatever way he can,
not too late,
not too soon.

He sits, waiting.
He doesn't know
why he should
have such a patience.

He sits at a table
on a chair.
He is comfortable
sitting there.

No one else
in this room,
no others, no expectations,
no sounds.

Had he walked
another way,
would he be here,
like they say.

Black Grackle

FOR STAN AND JANE

Black grackle's refreshing eyeblink
at kitchen sink's
wedged window —
a long way to go after all,

a long way back to the crack
in some specific wall
let the light in, so
to speak — Let the bird *speak,*

squeak prettily, and sit
on my finger, pecking ring's blue
stone. Home, home all around here,
geese peer in, goats graze, I suppose

they eat, want no
arbitrary company nor summary
investigation pretends in any way
so to know them — and give milk.

Youth has its own rewards,
and miles to go before I sleep
is echo of miles and miles,
wherever, whatever it was—

I wanted you and *you*
sat down to stay awhile.
If all there was was such
one pulled the threads and all

fell out, if going there was only
coming here with times between
and *everyday a holiday with Mary*
and *I love you still and always will,*

then *then* could not begin again
its busyness, its casual consequences,
and no head on no shoulders, *no*
eyes or ears, etc., nothing forward

in this peculiarly precious instance
scrunched down here, screaming—ultimate *me*—
for miles and miles around
its devastating sound.

The Seasons

FOR JASPER JOHNS

"Therefore all seasons will be sweet to thee . . ."
— S. T. COLERIDGE, "FROST AT MIDNIGHT"

Was it *thunk* suck
of sound an insistent

outside into the patience
abstract waited was lost

in such simple flesh *où*
sont les mother and

father so tall the green
hills echoéd and light

was longer, longer, into
the sun, all the small

body bent at last to
double back into one

and one and one wonder,
paramour pleasure.

      •

High air's lightness heat
haze grasshopper's chirr

sun's up hum two close
wet sweat time's hung in space

dust deep greens a wave of grasses
smells grow faint sounds echo

the hill again up and down
we go—

summer, summer, and not even
the full of it . . .

Echoes again body's time a
ticking a faint insistent

intimate skin wants weather
to reassure.

     .

All grown large world
round *ripeness is all*

an orange pumpkin harsh
edge now of frost an

autumnal moon over the
far off field leads back

to the house all's dead
silence the peculiarly

constructed one you were
all by yourself   *Shine on*

Hear the walls of fall
The dark flutes of autumn

sound softly . . . Oh love,
love, remember me.

     .

As if because or
whenever it was it was

there again muffled mute
an extraordinary quiet

white and cold far off
hung in the air without

apparent edge or end
nowhere one was or if

then gone waited
come full circle again

deep and thick and even
again and again

having thought to go nowhere
had got there.

    ·

The seasons, tallies of earth,
keep count of time,
say what it's worth.

Sight

Eye's reach out window water's
lateral quiet bulk of trees at
far edge now if peace were
possible here it would enter.

    ·

Bulk of trees' tops mass of
substantial trunks supporting from
shifting green base lawn variable
greens and almost yellow looks like.

    ·

Seven grey metal canoes drawn
up and tethered by pond's long
side with brushy green bushes and
metallic light sheen of water at evening.

.

What see what look for what
seems to be there front of the fore-
head the echoing painful minded-
ness of life will not see this here.

Four
DREAMS

Dreams

What you think you
eat at some table like
a pig with people
you don't even

know and lady there
feeds you all and you,
finally you at least
are full, say, look at

them still eating! Why
(says a woman, another
sitting next to me) those
others still eating you

so cannily observed are
unlike you who *could* be fed
because you were hungry! But
them, they can't—they

are possessed by the
idea of hunger, *never* enough
to eat for them, agh . . .
Or you either, dreamer,

who tells this simple
story being all these
same offensive persons
in one empty head.

.

In dreams begin the
particulars of those
echoes and edges,

the quaint ledges of
specific childhood nailed
to my knees and

leaning in unison
while the other
men went off, the

women working, the
kids at baleful
play, mud-colored

with rocks and stones and
trees years ago in
Albuquerque, New Mexico we'd

stopped the night I dreamt
I was to be child forever
on way to get the kids from camp.

      ·

Have you ever
had vision as if

you were walking
forward to some

edge of water through
the trees, some country

sunlit lane, some
place was just ahead

and opening as your body
elsewise came

and you had
been in two places?

For the World That Exists

No safer place to live than with children
for the world that exists.

If

Up the edge of the window out to
tree's overhanging branches sky
light on facing building up to
faint wash blue up on feet ache
now old toes wornout joints make
the wings of an angel so I'd fly.

Lights

I could get
all of it.

I could say
anything.

I wish I could
just get even.

I'm here.
I'm still here.

When did
it happen.

Where was
everyone.

I wish I could
just get even.

Now you've
gone away.

Nobody
wants to stay.

Here I am.
Here I am.

I Dreamt

I dreamt I dwelt in a big building—
four walls, floor and a ceiling,
bars in front and behind.
Nothing on my mind.

I dreamt I dwelt in a can,
round, tin, sides, top and bottom,
and I couldn't get out.
Nobody to get me out.

I dreamt I dwelt in marble halls,
a men's room with a trough
you pissed in, and there I was.
There were a lot of us.

I dreamt I dwelt in a house,
a home, a heap of living
people, dogs, cats, flowers.
It went on for hours.

Whatever you dream is true.
It's just you making it up,
having nothing better to do.
Even if you wanted to, you couldn't.

Sparks Street Echo

Flakes falling
out window make
no place, no place—

no faces, traces,
wastes of whatever
wanted to be—

was here
momently, mother,
was here.

You

You were leaving, going
out the door in

preoccupation as to
what purpose it

had served, what
the point was, even

who or what or where,
when you thought you

could, suddenly, say
you understood, and

saw all people as if
at some distance, a

pathetic, vast huddle
up against a fence.

You were by no means
the Cosmic Farmer

nor Great Eyeball in Sky.
You were tired, old now,

confused as to purpose,
even finally alone.

You walked slowly
away or rather got in

the car was waiting
with the others.

How to say clearly what
we think so matters

is bullshit, how all the
seeming difference is none?

Would they listen, presuming
such a *they?* Is any-

one ever home to such in-
sistences? How ring

the communal bell?
All was seen in

a common mirror, all
was simple self-

reflection. It was me
and I was you.

Focus

Patches of grey
sky tree's

lines window
frames the

plant hangs
in middle.

Plague

When the world has become a pestilence,
a sullen, inexplicable contagion,

when men, women, children
die in no sense realized, in

no time for anything, a
painful rush inward, isolate —

as when in my childhood the
lonely leper pariahs so seemingly

distant were just down the street,
back of drawn shades, closed doors —

no one talked to them, no one
held them anymore, no one waited

for the next thing to happen — as
we think now the day begins

again, as we look for the faint sun,
as they are still there, we hope, and we are coming.

Age

Most explicit—
the sense of trap

as a narrowing
cone one's got

stuck into and
any movement

forward simply
wedges one more—

but where
or quite when,

even with whom,
since now there is no one

quite with you—   Quite? Quiet?
English expression: *Quait?*

Language of singular
impedance? A dance? An

involuntary gesture to
others *not* there? What's

wrong here? How
reach out to the

other side all
others live on as

now you see the
two doctors, behind

you, in mind's eye,
probe into your anus,

or ass, or bottom,
behind you, the roto-

rooter-like device
sees all up, concludes

"like a worn out inner tube,"
"old," prose prolapsed, person's

problems won't do, must
cut into, cut out . . .

The world is a round but
diminishing ball, a spherical

ice cube, a dusty
joke, a fading,

faint echo of its
former self but remembers,

sometimes, its past, sees
friends, places, reflections,

talks to itself in a fond,
judgmental murmur,

alone at last.
I stood so close

to you I could have
reached out and

touched you just
as you turned

over and began to
snore not unattractively,

no, never less than
attractively, my love,

my love—but in this
curiously glowing dark, this

finite emptiness, *you, you, you*
are crucial, hear the

whimpering back of
the talk, the approaching

fears when I may
cease to be me, all

lost or rather lumped
here in a retrograded,

dislocating, imploding
self, a uselessness

talks, even if finally to no one,
talks and talks.

Funny

Why isn't it funny when you die,
at least lapse back into archaic pattern,
not the peculiar holding on to container
all other worlds were thought to be in—

archaic, curious ghost story then,
all sitting in the familiar circle,
the light fading out at the edges,
and voices one thinks are calling.

You watch them go first, one by one,
you hold on to the small, familiar places,
you love intently, wistfully, now
all that you've been given.

But you can't be done with it
and you're by no means alone.
You're waiting, watching them go,
know there's an end to it.

Five
EIGHT PLUS

Improvisations

FOR LISE HOSHOUR

YOU BET
Birds like
windows.

·

YONDER
Heaven's up
there still.

·

THE KIDS
Little
muffins

in a
pan.

·

THE CART
Oh well, it
thinks.

·

NEGATIVE
There's a big
hole.

·

SITE
Slats in
sunlight a
shadow.

     •

PURITAN
Plant's in
place.

     •

VIRTUES
Tree limbs'
patience.

     •

CARS
Flat out
parking lot.

     •

BLUE
Grey blue
sky blue.

     •

HOLES
Sun's
shining through

you.

     •

TEXAS REVERSE
You all
go.

•

ECHOES
"All god's
children got—"

•

OLD SONG
"Some sunny
day—"

•

YEAH
Amazing grace
on Willy's face!

•

HELP
This here
hand's out.

•

SEE
Brown's another
color.

•

DOWN
It's all
over
the floor.

•

WINDOW
Up from reflective
table top's glass the
other side of it.

.

AROUND
The pinwheel's pink
plastic spinning
blade's reversing.

.

EGO
I can
hear I can
see.

.

DAYTIME
It's got to be
lighter.

.

SPACE
Two candles
light brown—
or yellow?

.

WINDOW SEAT
Cat's up
on chair's edge.

.

EYES
All this
color's yours.

.

GREEN
Plant's tendrils
hanging from

but not
to—

.

SEASCAPE
Little boat
blue blown
by bay.

.

BIT
"De
sign Qu
art
e[a]rly"

.

GROUP
"AL
APHIC
Y"

.

WEIGH
Rippled refractive
surface leaves
light lights.

.

THE EDGE
"Your
Mem
Is Enc

.

QUOTE
"a lot
of thought-
ful people"

.

GHOST
What you don't
see you
hear?

.

TEACHER
The big
red
apple.

.

CANDLE HOLDER
Small glass
cube's opaque
clarity in
window's light.

·

FIELDS
Meadows
more at home.

·

TABLE TOP
Persian's
under glass.

Wheels

FOR FUTURA 2000

One around one—
or inside, limit
and dispersal.

Outside, the emptiness
of no edge, round
as the sky—

Or the eye seeing
all go by
in a blur of silence.

Oh

Oh stay awhile,
sad, sagging flesh
and bones gone brittle.

Stay in place,
agèd face, teeth,
don't go.

Inside and out
the flaccid change
of bodily parts,

mechanics of action,
mind's collapsing
habits, all

echo here
in mottled skin, blurred eye,
reiterated mumble.

Lift to the vacant air
some sigh, some sign
I'm still inside.

Reading of Emmanuel Levinas

"He does not limit knowledge
nor become the object of thinking . . ."

— KRZYSTZTOF ZIAREK

Thought out of self
left beyond the door

left out at night
shuttered openness

dreams dream of dreaming
inside seeming outside

since left then gone
comes home alone.

·

Puts hands down
no river one place

step over into
the ground sense

place was will be
here and now

nowhere can be
nothing's left.

·

Outside forms distance
some hundred feet

away in boxed air across
bricked enclosed space

a horizontal young woman
blue coat red pants

asleep on couch seen
through squared window

five floors up in form
above's blue sky

a lateral cloud
air of solemn thinking.

     .

Who else was
when had they come

what was the program
who was one

why me there
what other if

the place was determined
the deed was done?

Water

Your personal world echoes
in ways common enough,
a parking lot, common cold,
the others sitting at the table.

I have no thoughts myself,
more than myself. I feel
here enough now to think
at least I am here.

So you should get to
know me? Would I be
where you looked? Is it
hands across this body of water?

Is anyone out there,
they used to say, or was
they also some remote chance
of people, a company, together.

What one never knows is,
is it really real, is
the obvious obvious, or else
a place one lives in regardless.

Consolatio

What's gone is gone.
What's lost is lost.

What's felt as pulse —
what's mind, what's home.

Who's here, where's there —
what's patience now.

What thought of all,
why echo it.

Now to begin —
Why fear the end.

What

What would it be
like walking off
by oneself down

that path in the
classic woods the light
lift of breeze softness

of this early evening and
you want some time
to yourself to think

of it all again
and again an
empty ending?

Senator Blank Blank

I look at your
bland, piglike
face and hear

your thin-lipped,
rhetorical bullshit
and wonder if anyone

can or will believe you,
and know they do,
just that I'm listening to you too.

Better

Would it be better
piecemeal, a little
now and then, or

could one get inside
and hide there, wait
for it to end.

No one's doing anything to you.
It's just there's nothing
they can do for you.

Better with dignity to die?
Better rhetoric would clarify.
"Better Business Bureaus" lie.

Wall

You can push as hard as you want
on this outside side.

It stays limited
to a single face.

USA

Seeing with Sidney people
asleep on floor of subway—

myself worrying about time—
how long it would take to get to the plane—

How far in the universe to get home,
what do you do when you're still alone,

what do you say when no one asks,
what do you want you don't take—

When train finally comes in,
there's nothing you're leaving, nothing you can.

For an Old Friend

What became of your novel with the lunatic
mistaken for an undercover agent,

of your investment of the insistently vulnerable
with a tender of response,

your thoughtful wish that British letters
might do better than Peter Russell—

Last time I saw you, protesting
in London railway station

that all was changed,
you asked for a tenner

to get back to Bexhill-on-Sea.
Do you ever think of me.

Here

In other
words opaque
disposition intended
for no one's interest
or determination
forgotten ever
increased but
inflexible and
left afterwards.

Ears Idle Ears

FOR SUSAN

Out one
ear and
in the
other ear
and out
without it.

Blue Moon

The chair's still there,
but the goddamn sun's
gone red again—

and instead of Mabel
there is a potato,
or something like that there,

sitting like it owned the place.
It's got no face
and it won't speak to anyone.

I'm scared.
If I had legs,
I'd run.

Echo

Rudimentary characteristic of being
where it has to be, this tree

was where it was
a long time before anything else

I know or thought to.
Now it's pushed out by people—

rather by their effects, the weakening
the insistent wastes produce.

Where can anyone go
finally if the damn trees die

from what's done to them—what
being so-called *alive* has come to?

What's left after such death.
If nothing's there, who's here.

Famous Last Words

FOR JOHN CHAMBERLAIN

PLACE
There's a way out
of here but it

hurts at the edges
where there's no time left

to be one if
you were and friends

gone, days seemingly
over. No one.

·

LATE
Looks like chunks
will be it

tonight, a bite-sized
lunch of love,

and lots of it,
honey.

·

VERDE
Green, how I love you green . . .
the prettiest color I've ever seen,

the way to the roses through them stems,
the way to go when the light changes!

What grass gets when you water it,
or the folding stuff can get you in,

but finally it's what isn't dead
unless it's skin with nothing under it—

or faces green from envy or hunger or fear,
or some parallel biological fact, my dear.

·

BOZO
Bill's brother was partial
to windows, stood on boxes

looking over their edges.
His head was

higher than his shoulders,
but his eyes were

somewhere down under
where he thought he could

see it all now, all
he'd wanted to, aged four,

looking up under skirts,
wearing ochre-trim western shirts.

Regular slim-jim ranchero,
this vicious, ambitious, duplicitous, no

wish too late, too
small, bozo.

.

MILES
Simple trips, going
places, wasted
feelings, alone
at last, all the rest

of it, counting, keeping
it together, the weather,
the particular people, all
the ways you have to.

.

NIGHT LIGHT
Look at the light
between the lights

at night with the lights
on in the room you're sitting

in alone again with
the light on trying still

to sleep but bored and
tired of waiting up late

at night thinking of some
stupid simple sunlight.

.

ECHOES (1)
Patience, a peculiar
virtue, waits in time,

depends on time to
make it, thinks it

can have everything
it wants, wants all

of it and echoes dis-
appointment, thinks

of what it thought
it wanted, nothing else.

.

ECHOES (2)
This intensive going in,
to live there, in

the head, to wait
for what it seems

to want, to look
at all the ways

of looking, seeing
things, to always

think of it, think
thinking's going to work.

.

LIFE
All the ways to go,
the echoes, made sense.

It was as fast as that,
no time to figure it out.

No simple straight line,
you'd get there in time

enough standing still.
It came to you

whatever you planned to do.
Later, you'd get it together.

Now it was here.
Time to move.

.

FAMOUS LAST WORDS
Which way did they go?
Which way did they come.

If it's not fun, don't do it.
But I'm sure you wouldn't.

You can sum it all up in a few words
or less if you want to save time.

No wisdom hasn't been worn out
by simple repetition.

You'll be with me till the end?
Good luck, friend.

Echoes

FOR WILLIAM BRONK

The stars stay up there where they first were.
We have changed but they seem as ever.

What was their company first to be, their curious proposal,
that we might get there which, of course, we did.

How dead now the proposal of life simply, how echoing it is,
how everything we did, we did and thought we did!

Was it always you as one, and them as one,
and one another was us, we thought, a protestant, a complex

determination of this loneliness of human spaces.
What could stars be but something else no longer there,

some echoing light too late to be for us specific.
But there they were and there we saw them.

Eight Plus

Inscriptions for Eight Bollards
at 7th & Figueroa, LA

FOR JAMES SURLS

What's still here settles
at the edges of this
simple place still
waiting to be seen.

·

I didn't go
anywhere and
I haven't
come back!

·

You went by so
quickly thinking
there's a whole world
in between.

．

It's not a
final distance,
this here
and now.

．

How much I would
give just to know
you're standing in
whatever way here.

．

Human eyes
are lights to me
sealed
in this stone.

．

No way to
tell you anything
more than
this one.

．

You walk tired
or refreshed, are
past in a moment,
but saw me.

．

Wish happiness
most for us,
whoever we are,
wherever.

·

If I sit here
long enough,
all will pass me by
one way or another.

·

Nothing left out,
it's all in a heap,
all the people
completed.

·

Night's eye is
memory
in day-
light.

·

I've come and gone from here
with no effect,
and now feel
no use left.

·

How far from
where it
was I'll
never know.

·

You there
next to the others
in front of
the one behind!

          .

No one speaks
alone. It
comes out
of something.

          .

Could I think
of all you
must have felt?
Tell me.

          .

What's inside,
what's the place
apart from
this one?

          .

They say this
used to be
a forest
with a lake.

          .

I'm just
a common
rock,
talking.

          .

World's
still got
four
corners.

.

What's
that
up there
looking down?

.

You've got a nice
face and
kind eyes and
all the trimmings.

.

We talk like
this too
often someone
will get wise!

Six

HELSINKI WINDOW

"Even if he were to throw out by now absolutely incomprehensible stuff about the burning building and look upon his work simply as an effort of a carpenter to realize a blueprint in his mind, every morning he wakes up and goes to look at his house, it is as if during the night invisible workmen had been monkeying with it, a stringer has been made away with in the night and mysteriously replaced by one of inferior quality, while the floor, so meticulously set by a spirit level the night before, now looks as if it had not even been adjudged by setting a dish of water on it, and cants like the deck of a steamer in a gale. It is for reasons analogous to this perhaps that short poems were invented, like perfectly measured frames thrown up in an instant of inspiration and, left to suggest the rest, in part manage to outwit the process."

– MALCOLM LOWRY, *DARK AS THE GRAVE WHEREIN MY FRIEND IS LAID*

X

The trees are kept
in the center of the court,
where they take up room
just to prove it—

and the garbage cans extend
on the asphalt at the far side
under the grey sky and the building's
recessed, regular windows.

All these go up and down
with significant pattern,
and people look out of them.
One can see their faces.

I know I am safe here
and that no one will get me,
no matter where it is
or who can find me.

Help

Places one's come to
in a curious stumble, things
one's been put to, with,
in a common bundle

called suffering humanity
with faces, hands
where they ought to be,
leaving usual bloody traces.

I like myself, he thought, but
it was years and years ago
he could stand there watching
himself like a tv show.

Now you're inside entirely,
he whispers in mock self-reassurance,
because he recognizes at last, by god,
he's not all there is.

Small Time

Why so curiously happy
with such patient small agony
not hurting enough
to be real to oneself—

or even intimidated
that it's at last too late
to make some move
toward something else.

Late sun, late sun,
this far north you still shine,
and it's all fine,
and there's still time enough.

Bienvenu

FOR THE COMPANY
OF LISE HOSHOUR, PHILIPPE BRIET,
MICHEL BUTOR, AND ROBERT THERRIEN:
"7&6," PHILIPPE BRIET GALLERY,
NYC, OCTOBER 7, 1988

Welcome to this bienfait
ministry of interior muses,
thoughtful provocateurs, etc.

All that meets your eye
you'll hear with ear
of silent surprises

and see these vast surmises
bien entendu by each
autre autrefois. Our

welcome so to you
has come—Mon frère, mon semblable,
and sisters all.

.

Thoughtful little holes in
places makes us
be here.

Empty weather makes
a place of faces
staring in.

Come look at
what we three
have done here.

"Ever Since Hitler . . ."

Ever since Hitler
or well before that
fact of human appetite
addressed with brutal
indifference others
killed or tortured or ate
the same bodies they
themselves had we ourselves
had plunged into density
of selves all seeming stinking
one no possible way
out of it smiled or cried
or tore at it and died
apparently dead at last
just no other way out.

Thinking

I've thought of myself
as objective, viz.,
a thing round which
lines could be drawn —

or else placed by years, the average
some sixty, say, a relative
number of months, days,
hours and minutes.

I remember thinking of war
and peace and life
for as long as I can remember.
I think we were right.

But it changes, it thinks
it can all go on forever
but it gets older.
What it wants is rest.

I've thought of place
as how long it takes
to get there and of where
it then is.

I've thought of clouds, of water
in long horizontal bodies, or
of love and women and the children
which came after.

Amazing what mind makes
out of its little pictures,
the squiggles and dots,
not to mention the words.

Clouds

The clouds passing over, the
wisps still seeming substantial, as
a kid, as a kid I'd see them up there

in the town I grew up in on the hills
in the fields on the way home then
as now still up there, still up there.

All Wall

Vertical skull time
weather blast bombastic disaster impasse time,
like an inside out and back down again design,
despair ready wear impacted beware scare time—

like old Halloween time,
people all gone away and won't be back time,
no answer weeks later empty gone out dead
a minute ahead of your call just keeps on ringing time—

I'm can't find my way back again time,
I'm sure it was here but now I can't find it time,
I'm a drag and sick and losing again wasted time,
You're the one can haul me out and start it over again

Time. Too much time too little
not enough too much still to go time,
and time after time and not done yet time
nothing left time to go time. Time.

Whatever

Whatever's
to be
thought
of thinking
thinking's
thought of
it still
thinks
it thinks
to know
itself so
thought.

.

Thought so
itself know to
thinks it
thinks still it
of thought
thinking's
thinking
of thought
be to
whatever's.

Klaus Reichert and Creeley Send Regards

IN MEMORY L. Z.

Nowhere up there enough
apart as surmised see my
ears feel better in the
air an after word from Romeo's
delight spells *the* and *a*
aged ten forever friend
you'll know all this by heart.

Echoes

What kind of crows,
grey and black, fussy
like jays, flop
on the tree branches?

"What kind of
love is this" flops
flat nightly, sleeps
away the days?

What kind of place
is this? What's out there
in these wet unfamiliar
streets and flattened,

stretched faces?
Who's been left here,
what's been wasted
again.

Fools

1

Stripped trees in the wet wind,
leaves orange yellow, some still green,
winter's edge in the air,
the close, grey sky . . .

Why not be more
human, as they say,
more thoughtful,
why not try to care.

The bleak alternative's
a stubborn existence —
back turned to all,
pathetic resistance.

2

You'd think the fact
another's tried it
in the common world
might be a language

like the animals
seem to know
where they've come from
and where they'll go.

Curse the fool
who closes his sad door —
or any other more
still tries to open it.

Meat

Blood's on the edge of it
the man with the knife cuts into it

the way out is via the door to it
the moves you have mean nothing to it

but you can't get away from it
there's nothing else left but it

have you had enough of it
you won't get away from it

this room is thick with it
this air smells of it

your hands are full of it
your mouth is full of it

why did you want so much of it
when will you quit it

all this racket is still it
all that sky is it

that little spot is it
what you still can think of is it

anything you remember is it
all you ever got done is always it

your last words will be it
your last wish will be it

The last echo it last faint color it
the drip the trace the stain—it.

New Year's Resolution

What one might say
wanting to do it,
hoping to solve it,
make resolution —

You break it to bits,
swallow the pieces,
finally quit quitting,
accept it, forget it.

But what world is this
has such parts,
or makes even thinkable
paradoxic new starts —

Turn of the year
weighs in the cold
all that's proposed
simply to change it.

Still, try again
to be common, human,
learn from all
how to be one included.

The Drunks of Helsinki

Blue sky, a lurching tram makes
headway through the small city.
The quiet company sits shyly,
avoiding its image, else talks

with securing friends. This
passage is through life as if
in dream. We know our routes
and mean to get there. Now

the foetid stink of human excess,
plaintive, and the person beside us
lurches, yet stays stolidly there.
What are the signals? Despair,

loss of determinants – or a world
just out of a bottle? Day
after day they clutter the tram
stops, fall sodden over seats

and take their drunken ease in
the fragile world. I think, they
are the poets, the maledictive,
muttering words, fingers pointing,

pointing, jabbed outright across
aisle to blank side of bank or
the company's skittish presence.
I saw a man keep slamming the post

with his fist, solid in impact,
measured blows. His semblable sat
slumped in front of me, a single seat.
They meet across the aisle in ranting voices,

each talking alone. In a place of
so few words sparely chosen, their
panegyric slabbering whine has human
if unexpected resonance. They

speak for us, their careful friends, the sober
who scuttle from side to side in vacantly
complex isolation, in a company has compact
consensus, minds empty of all conclusion.

Helsinki Window

FOR ANSELM HOLLO

Go out into brightened
space out there the fainter
yellowish place it
makes for eye to enter out
to greyed penumbra all the
way to thoughtful searching
sight of all beyond that
solid red both brick and seeming
metal roof or higher black
beyond the genial slope I
look at daily house top on
my own way up to heaven.

.

Same roof, light's gone
down back of it, behind
the crying end of day, "I
need something to do," it's
been again those other
things, what's out there,
sodden edge of sea's
bay, city's graveyard, park
deserted, flattened aspect,
leaves gone colored fall
to sidewalk, street, the end
of all these days but
still this regal light.

.

Trees stripped, rather shed
of leaves, the black solid trunks up
to fibrous mesh of smaller
branches, it is weather's window,
weather's particular echo, here
as if this place had been once,
now vacant, a door that had had
hinges swung in air's peculiar
emptiness, greyed, slumped elsewhere,
asphalt blank of sidewalks, line of
linearly absolute black metal fence.

                    .

Old sky freshened with cloud bulk
slides over frame of window the
shadings of softened greys a light
of air up out of this dense high
structured enclosure of buildings
top or pushed up flat of bricked roof
frame I love *I love* the safety of
small world this door frame back
of me the panes of simple glass yet
airy up sweep of birch trees sit in
flat below all designation declaration
here as clouds move so simply away.

                    .

Windows now lit close out the
upper dark the night's a face
three eyes far fainter than
the day all faced with light
inside the room makes eye re-
flective see the common world
as one again no outside coming

in no more than walls and post-
card pictures place faces across
that cautious dark the tree no
longer seen more than black edge
close branches somehow still between.

     •

He was at the edge of this
reflective echo the words blown
back in air a bubble of suddenly
apparent person who walked to
sit down by the familiar brook and
thought about his fading life
all "fading life" in tremulous airy
perspect saw it hover in the surface
of that moving darkness at the edge
of sun's passing water's sudden depth
his own hands' knotted surface the
sounding in himself of some other.

     •

One forty five afternoon red
car parked left hand side
of street no distinguishing
feature still wet day a bicycle
across the way a green door-
way with arched upper window
a backyard edge of back wall
to enclosed alley low down small
windows and two other cars green
and blue parked too and miles
and more miles still to go.

     •

This early still sunless morning when a chair's
creak translates to cat's cry a blackness still
out the window might be apparent night when the
house still sleeping behind me seems a bag of
immense empty silence and I feel the children
still breathing still shifting their dreams an
enigma will soon arrive here and the loved one
centers all in her heavy sleeping arm out the
leg pushed down bedclothes this body unseen un-
known placed out there in night I can feel all
about me still sitting in this small spare pool of
light watching the letters the words try to speak.

.

Classic emptiness it
sits out there edge of
hierarchic roof top it
marks with acid fine edge
of apparent difference it
is *there* here *here* that
sky so up and out and where
it wants to be no birds no
other thing can for a
moment distract it be
beyond its simple space.

What

What had one thought the
outside was but place all
evident surface and each
supposed perspect touched
texture all the wet implicit
world was adamant edge of

limit responsive if indifferent
and changing (one thought) in-
side its own evident kind one
banged upon abstract insens-
itive else echoed in passing
was it the movement one's own?

Voice

Bears down on
the incisive way to
make a point common
enough speaking
in various terms it
says the way of
satisfaction is a
lowly thing echo
even wants to can
come along alone in-
clusion also a way
particularizing life.

So Much

When he was a kid sick
in bed out the window
the clouds were thick and
like castles, battlements he'd
think he could climb up to
them, a veritable jack in
the beanstalk high there with

sun and blue air he'd never
need anything more again to
get well, so it had to fade
away, whatever that old voice
enlarges, so much to depend upon.

Echo

FOR J. L.

Outside the
trees
make limit of
simple

sight. The
weather is
a grey, cold on
the

skin. It feels
itself
as if a place it
couldn't

ever get to
had been at
last
entered.

Winter Night

Buildings high bulk lifts
up the mass is lighter in this
curiously illumined darkness air
somehow fragile with the light is
beyond again in yellow lit win-
dows frame of the bars and behind
a seeming room the lamp on the
table there such peculiar small
caring such signs five floors up
or out window see balcony's iron
frame against snowed roof's white
or pinkish close glow all beyond.

Fading Light

Now one might catch it see it
shift almost substantial blue
white yellow light near roof's edge
become intense definition think
of the spinning world is it as
ever this plate of apparent life
makes all sit patient hold on
chute the sled plunges down ends
down the hill beyond sight down
into field's darkness as time for
supper here left years behind waits
patient in mind remembers the time.

Old Mister Moonlight

Split broken un-
circumvented excised
walked out door snow
day freaking thoughts
of empty memory back
past time gone undone
left car side pool
of greying edged
rings fledged things
wedged buildings all
patterns and plans fixed
focus death again.

For J. L.

The ducks are gone
back to the pond, the echo

of it all a curious
resonance now it's

over, life's like that?
What matters, so soon become fact.

Night

This bluish light behind the block of
building this familiar returning
night comes closer this way can sit
looking see the bulk of it take shape
in front of the sky comes now up from

behind it up to mount its light its
yellow quiet squares fix a front in
the dark to be there make a static
place looks like home in dark's
ambivalence sit down to stay awhile
places there black's dominance a shade it
rides to closes it shuts it finally off.

March

Almost at the dulled
window fact the wet
birches soften in melt-
ing weather up still from
far ground the backyard
asphalt grey plastic garbage
bins the small squat
blackened pile of stubborn
snow still sit there echo
of fading winter all the days
we waited for this side
of spring changes everything.

First Love

Oh your face is there a mirror days
weeks we lived those other places in
all that ridiculous waste the young we
wanted not to be walked endless streets
in novels read about life went home at
night to sleep in tentative houses left

one another somewhere now unclear no per-
sons really left but for paper a child or
two or three and whatever physical events
were carved then on that tree like initials
a heart a face of quiet blood and somehow
you kept saying and saying an unending pain.

Spring Light

Could persons be as this
fluffed light golden spaces
intent airy distances so up
and out again they are here
the evening lowers against the sun
the night waits far off at the
edge and back of dark is summer's
light that slanting clarity all
wonders come again the bodies open
stone stillness stunned in the silence
hovering waiting touch of air's edge
piece of what had not been lost.

Echoes

. . . Sea, hill and wood,
This populous village! Sea, and hill, and wood,
With all the numberless goings on of life,
Inaudible as dreams! the thin-blue flame
Lies on my low-burnt fire, and quivers not;
Only that film, which fluttered on the grate,
Still flutters there, the sole unquiet thing.
Methinks, its motion in this hush of nature
Gives it dim sympathies with me who live,
Making it a companionable form,
Whose puny flaps and freaks the idling Spirit
By its own moods interprets, every where
Echo or mirror seeking of itself,
And makes a toy of Thought.

— S. T. COLERIDGE,
"FROST AT MIDNIGHT"

One

My New Mexico

FOR GUS BLAISDELL

Edge of door's window
sun against
flat side adobe,
yellowed brown—

A blue lifting morning,
miles of spaced echo,
time here plunged
backward, backward—

I see shadowed leaf
on window frame green,
close plant's growth,
weathered fence slats—

All passage explicit,
the veins, hands,
lined faces crease,
determined—

Oh sun! Three years,
when I came first,
it had shone unblinking,
sky vast aching blue—

The sharpness of each
shift the pleasure,
pain, of particulars—
All inside gone out.

Sing me a song
makes beat specific,
takes the sharp air,
echoes this silence.

Brick

Have I bricked up unbricked what
perspective hole break of eye
seen what glowing place what
flower so close grows from a
tiny brown seed or was it what
I wanted this after imaged green
round sun faints under blue sky
or outer space that place no
one knows but for this echo of
sketched in color the stems of
the voluptuous flowers patient
myself inside looking still out.

Bowl

He comes she comes carrying carrying
a flower an intense interest a color
curious placed in an outer an inner
ring of rounded spaces of color it
looked this way they say it was here
and there it was it opened opens color
it sees itself seen faithful to echo
more than all or was the green seeming
back of it fragile shoots a way it was
yellow banded together zigzagged across
as a box for it wants to touch touches
opens at the edges a flower in a bowl.

Shadow

There is a shadow
to intention a place
it comes through and
is itself each stasis
of its mindedness ex-
plicit walled into
semblance it is a
seemingly living place
it wants it fades it
comes and goes it puts
a yellow flower in a pot
in a circle and looks.

Figure of Fun

Blue dressed aged blonde
person with pin left
lapel hair bulged to
triangular contained wide
blue grey eyed now
authority prime minister
of aged realm this
hallowed hollowed ground
lapped round with salted water
under which a tunnel runs
to far off France and history
once comfortably avoided.

Waldoboro Eve

Trees haze in the fog coming in,
late afternoon sun still catches the stones.

Dog's waiting to be fed by the empty sink,
I hear the people shift in their rooms.

That's all finally there is to think.
Now comes night with the moon and the stars.

Old

Framed roof slope from tower's window
out to grey wet field with green growth,
edge again of midfield hedgerow and trees beyond,
the tugging familiar, the fading off fogged distance—

Are these memories already?
Does it seem to me I see what's there.
Have I particulars still to report,
is my body myself only?

Hear the cricket, the keening slight
sound of insect, the whirring of started
vacuum cleaner, television's faint voices now
down below. Here is world.

Old Words

The peculiar *fuck it*
cunt shit violence
of a past learned in
school all words only
one by one first heard
never forgotten as recall
head or heart vagaries
a dusk now so early
in the afternoon the wet
feel of days socks touch
of things said to me
forever please *fuck me.*

Translation

You have all the time been
here if not seen, not thought
of as present, for when I
looked I saw nothing, when
I looked again, you had
returned. This echo, sweet
spring, makes a human sound
you have no need of, facts
so precede, but you hear, you
hear it, must feel the intent
wetness, mushy. I melt again
into your ample presence.

Self Portrait

This face was detachable
as blurred head itself
lifted from old bookcover
library yielded a faded
years ago image graced
now newspaper's rushed
impression static glossed
sentiment "life" a few hours
more to "live" till wrapped
tight round fresh loaf delivered
come home eaten comes to rest
on yesterday's garbage.

Here Again

He was walking
toward the other in-
viting him for-
ward now with an
eager antici-
pation he could rec-
ognize if not al-
together trust him-
self with any-
one else still
waiting also
to be met.

Echo

Entire memory
hangs tree
in mind to see
a bird be—

but now puts stutter
to work, shutters
the windows, shudders,
sits and mutters—

because can't
go back, still
can't get
out. Still can't.

Pure

Why is it *pure*
so defeats, makes
simple possibility
cringe in opposition —

That bubbling, mingled
shit with water
lifted from bathtub's
drain hole's no

stranger to me,
nor ever in mind
blurred image, words
won't say what's

asked of them. I
think the world I think,
wipe my relentless ass,
wash hands under faucet.

Eyes

I hadn't noticed that
building front had narrow
arrowlike division going
up it the stairwell at
top a crest like spearpoint
red roofed it glistens
with rain the top sharply

drawn horizontal roof edge lets
sky back there be a faint
blue a fainter white light
growing longer now higher
going off out of sight.

Some

You have not simply
insisted on yourself
nor argued
the irrelevance

of any one else. You
have always wanted
to be friends, to be
one of many.

Persuaded
life even
in its largeness
might be brought

to care, you
tried to make it
care, humble, illiterate,
awkward gestured.

So you thought,
as inevitable age approached,
some loved you,
some.

You waited for
some wind
to lift, some
thing to happen,

proving it finally,
making sense more
than the literal,
still separate.

Echo

White light blocked
impulse of repose like
Wouldn't you tell me
what you were doing   Couldn't
I go where you go   Faith
you kept secretly because it
had no other place to be   My
eyeball's simple hole wherein
'the gold gathered the
glow around it'   All you
said you wanted fainted
All the ways to say   No

There

Seeming act
of thought's
gagging

insight out
there's spasmodic
patience a wreck

car's hauled
now away
another day's

gone to hell
you know like
hangs out.

Here Only

Why does it cry so much
facing its determined despair—
As woman locked in cage—
child—or eyes only left to look—
Why—   What wanted—   Why is it
this way or that way thrashes
stubborn only in its absence—
It was never there—was only
here to be itself—here only this
one chance to be—   Cannot live
except it finds a place given—
Open to itself only as any—

It

Nothing there
in absence as,
unfelt, it
repeated itself—

I saw it,
felt it,
wanted
to belt it—

Oh love, you
watch, you
are so
"patient"—

Or what
word makes my
malice
more.

Death

Unlet things
static dying
die in common
pieces less
crescendo
be it simple

complex death
a physical
world again un-
ended unbegun to
any other world
be this one.

Here and Now

Never other than this unless
is counted sudden, demanded
sense of falling or a loud,
inexplicable yell just back
of ears, or if the tangible
seeming world rears up dis-
torted, bites hands that would
feed it, can feel no agreeable
sensation in the subject's hard-
ly learned vocabulary of social
moves, agreements, mores —
then up shit creek sans paddle.

Abstract

The inertia unexpected of
particular reference, it
wasn't where you said it
would be, where you looked
wasn't where it was! What
fact of common world is

presumed common? The
objectifying death of all
human person, the ground?
There you are and I look
to see you still, all
the distance still implacable.

The Cup

Who had thought
echo precedent,

shadow the seen
thing, action

reflective —
whose thought was

consequential,
itself an act, a

walking round rim
to see what's within.

Chain

Had they told you, you
were "four or more cells
joined end to end" the Latin,
catena, "a chain," the loop,
the running leap to actual
heaven spills at my stunned
feet, pours out the imprison-

ing threads of genesis,
oh light beaded necklace,
chain round my neck, my
inexorably bound birth, the sweet
closed curve of fading life?

East Street

Sense of the present
world out window, eye's
blurred testament

to "St Francis Xavier's
School," red brick
and grey cornices,

the snow, day old,
like thin, curdled milk,
God's will high

above on cross
at church top over
embedded small arches

and close, tiled
roof. The cars
parked, the accelerating

motor of one
goes by, the substantial
old birch, this

closer look—
path Dennis shoveled—
distraction of all report.

Baroque

Would you live your life spectrum
of fly sealed in amber block's
walk the patient fixed window see
days a measure of tired time a
last minute thought of whatever not
now remembered lift up sit down
then be reminded the dog is your
paradigm seven years to one all
reckoned think out muse on be sud-
denly outside the skin standing
upright pimpled distinction chilled
independence found finally only one?

For Nothing Else

For nothing else,
this for love

for what other
one is this

for love once
was and is

for love,
for love.

Parts

FOR SUSAN ROTHENBERG

HUMAN LEG GOAT LEG
Which the way echoed
previous cloven-hoofed
dark field faint formed
those *goat men leading her*
in physical earth's spring
jumps one-legged parallel
long walked thinned out
to sparse grounded skin
bones of what scale say
now goat transforms man
then man goat become
and dances dances?

SNAKE FISH BIRD
Archaic evolving thing
in all surface all beginning
not hair or any seeming simple
extension bring to mind pattern
of woven wetnesses waste a streak
of wonder of evil tokens the underneath
beside ground's depths spoken
low in sight soundless in height
look past reflection see the light
flash of finned ripple wing
this ancient *Fellow* follow
to weather, to water, to earth.

HORSE LEG DOG HEAD
Its mute uncute cutoff
inconsequent eye slot
centuries' habits accumulate
barks the determined dog
beside horse the leg the
walking length the patent
patient slight bent limb
long fetlock faith faint
included instructions placed
aside gone all to vacant
grass placed patiently thus
foot's function mind's trust.

DOG LEG WHEEL
Four to the round
repetitive inexorable
sound the wheel the whine
the wishes of dogs
that the world be real
that masters feel
that bones be found
somewhere in the black ground
in front or in back
before and behind
hub for a head bark's
a long way back. And on

GOAT'S EYE
Eye hole's peculiar framed
see you, want you, think
of eye out, lost last sight,
past goat thoughts, what
was it, when or why —
Or if still the stiff

hair, musk, the way
eye looks out, black
line contracted, head's skull
unstudied, steady,
it led to lust, follows
its own way down to dust.

DOG HEAD WITH RABBIT LEG
Break the elliptical
make the face deadpan tell
nothing to it smile for the
camera lie down and roll over
be in complex pieces for once
you ran the good race broke
down and what's left you
least of all can understand.
It was cold. It was hard.
Dogs barked. Rabbits ran.
It comes to such end,
friend. Such is being dead.

DOG HEAD WITH CRESCENT MOON
Harvested this head's
a manifest of place the
firmament's fundament.
Overhead sky's black night
in lieu of echoed moon
seems sounding out
a crescent crescendo
for a dog's life.
Barked bones soft
mouth's brought home
the arc again the light.
Waits patient for reward.

BIRD AND CALF

Peculiar patience is death
like an envelope a flap
a postulate you'd left a
space where it was and it
has gathered the outside
of its body in or just
flopped down dropped all
alternative forever waiting
for the plummeting streak
gets closer closer and
the god who cleans up things
puts death to work.

HORSES' BREATH

Had never known blue air's
faded fascination had never
seen or went anywhere never
was a horse unridden but on
one proverbial frosty morning
whilst going to the kitchen
I thought of our lives' opaque
addiction to distances to
all the endless riders etched
on those faint horizons and
nuzzled the mere idea of you—
swapped breath. *Oh love, be true!*

Two

White Fence/White Fence

(FOR PAUL STRAND'S PHOTOGRAPH "WHITE FENCE")

Particularizing "White
Fence" beyond which
the seeming

echoes of barn, house,
bright light flat
on foursquare

far building while
in closer view shades
darken the faint ground.

Yet *fence* as
image or word,
white or black, or

where place the person,
the absent,
in this ring of focus?

I come closer, see
in *there* the
wistful security,

all in apparent place,
the resonant design, diamond,
the *dark/light,*

the way all plays to pattern,
the longed for world
of common facts.

Then this *fence* again,
as if pasted on,
pushes out and across,

a static, determined
progress of detailing
edges, *American,* an

odd reason so forced
to be seen. It
cannot accommodate,

cannot let get past,
unaffected, any, *must* be
"White Fence."

East Street Again

FOR CARL RAKOSI

The tree stands clear in the weather
by the telephone pole, its stiff brother.
Hard to think which is the better,
given living is what we're here for
and that one's soon dead no matter.
Neither people nor trees live forever.
But it's a dumb thought, lacking other.
Only this passing faint snow now for tether—
mind's deadness, emptiness for pleasure—
if such a flat, faint echo can be measure.
So much is forgotten no matter.
You do what you can do, no better.

Sonnets

FOR KEITH AND ROSMARIE

Come round again the banal
belligerence almost a
flatulent echo of times
when still young the Sino
etc conflict starvation lists
of people without work or place
world so opaque and desperate
no one wanted even to
go outside to play even
with Harry Buddy who hit
me who I hit stood slugging
while they egged us on.

     .

While ignorant armies clash
bash while on the motorway
traffic backed up while they
stand screaming at each other
while they have superior
armaments so wage just
war while it all provokes
excuses alternatives money
time wasted go tell it
on the town dump deadend
avoidance of all you might
have lived with once.

     .

Someone told me to stand
up to whoever pushed me
down when talking walking
hand on friend's simple
pleasures thus abound when

one has fun with one
another said surrogate
God and planted lettuce
asparagus had horses cows
the farm down the road
the ground I grew up
on unwon unending.

•

I'd take all the learned
manner of rational un-
derstanding away leave
the table to stand on
its own legs the plates
to stick there the food
for who wants it the places
obvious and ample and
even in mind think it
could be other than an
argument a twisting
away tormented unless.

•

Me is finally unable having
as all seem to ended with
lost chances happily enough
missed the boat took them
all to hell on a whim
went over whatever precipice
but no luck just stupid
preoccupation common
fear of being overly hurt
by the brutal exigencies were
what pushed and pulled
me too to common cause.

•

So being old and wise and
unwanted left over from
teeth wearing hands wearing
feet wearing head wearing
clothes I put on take now
off and sleep or not or sit
this afternoon morning night
time's patterns look up at
stars overhead there what
do they mean but how useless
all violence how far away you
are from what you want.

.

Some people you just
know and recognize,
whether a need or fact,
a disposition at that
moment is placed,
you're home, a light
is in that simple
window forever— As if
people had otherwise always
to be introduced, told
you're ok— But here
you're home, so longed
for, so curiously
without question found.

Other

Having begun in thought there
in that factual embodied wonder
what was lost in the emptied lovers
patience and mind I first felt there
wondered again and again what for
myself so meager and finally singular
despite all issued therefrom whether
sister or mother or brother and father
come to love's emptied place too late
to feel it again see again first there
all the peculiar wet tenderness the care
of her for whom to be other was first fate.

Body

Slope of it,
hope of it—
echoes faded,
what waited

up late inside
old desires
saw through
the screwed importunities.

This regret?
Nothing's left.
Skin's old,
story's told—

but still touch,
selfed body,
wants other,
another mother

to him, her
insistent "sin"
he lets in
to hold him.

Selfish bastard,
headless catastrophe.
Sans tits, cunt,
wholly blunt—

fucked it up,
roof top, loving cup,
sweatered room,
old love's tune.

Age dies old,
both men and women cold,
hold at last no one,
die alone.

Body lasts forever,
pointless conduit,
floods in its fever,
so issues others parturient.

Through legs wide,
from common hole site,
aching information's dumb tide
rides to the far side.

"You Were Never Lovelier . . ."

FOR CLETUS

Inside that insistence —
small recompense — Persistence —
No sense in witless
thoughtlessness, no one

has aptitude for waiting —
hating, staying away later,
alone, left over, saw
them all going

without her (him), wanted
one for him (her)self, left
on the shelf, "them" become
fact of final indifference —

The theme is thoughtlessness,
the mind's openness, the
head's large holes, the gaps
in apparent thinking. So that

amorphic trucks drive through
you, mere, mired, if unmoved,
agency, left by the proposed "they"
to stay, alone of all that was.

The world is, or seems, entirely
an aggression, a running over, an
impossible conjunct of misfits
crash about, hurting one another.

No names please, no no one or someone.
Say goodbye to the nonexistent — never
having lived again or ever, mindless —
trucks, holes, clouds, call them —

those sounds of shapes in tides of space—
pillaging weather, shifting about one
or two or simply several again, an issue
only of surmise, a surprise of

sunset or sunrise, a day or two can't
think about or move out, or be again certain,
be about one's own business, be vanity's own simpleton,
simply, *You Were Never Lovelier . . .*

Reflection

It must be low key
breeze blowing through
room's emptiness is
something to think of—

but not enough
punch, pain enough,
despair to make
all else fade out—

This morning, that
morning? Another ample
day in the diminishing
possibility, the

reflective reality
alters to place
in specific place
what can't get past.

The Old Days

Implicit echo of the
seemingly friendly
face and grace as well
to be still said. Go to hell

(or heaven), old American
saying— My sister's friends
are affectionate people,
and also seemingly real.

Can I calculate—as to say,
can I still stay up late
enough to catch Santa Claus or
New Year's, are the small, still

tenets of truth still observable—
And how is your mother? Dead, sir,
these less than twenty years.
The voice echoes the way it was—

And if I am mistaken, sir.
If I am thought in error, was the error
intentional, did I mean to confuse you.
Were the great waves of myriad voices too

much of enough— You remember Cocteau's *A little
too much is enough for me*— Tits were beautiful—
bubbles of unstable flesh, pure, tilting pleasure.
You cannot finally abjure beauty

nor can you simply live without it—
reflective, beating your meat, unspeakable,
light headed with loneliness. Oh to be old
enough, fall down the stairs, break everything—

One often did but in such company
was heaven— Breath, arms, eyes,
and consummate softness— Breathing softness,
moist, simply conjoining softness, like a pillow.

No man is an island, no woman a pillow—
Nobody's anything anymore. Was it Pound
who said, *The way out is via the door*—
Do they say that anymore—

Do I hear what I hear. Then where
are the snows of yesteryear,
the face that sank a thousand ships,
all that comforting, nostalgic stuff

we used to hear. Sitting in company
with others, I look at the backs
of my hands, see slightly mottled,
swollen flesh, hear difficultly

through many voices—see a blur.
Yet you were, you are here—
If I am a fool in love,
you'll never leave me now.

Your

One sided
battering ramm'd
negligible asset
carnal friend—

Patience's provision
test of time
nothing ventured
nothing gained—

In the fat doldrums
of innocent aging
I sat waiting—
Thank god you came.

Gnomic Verses

LOOP
Down the road Up the hill Into the house
Over the wall Under the bed After the fact
By the way Out of the woods Behind the times
In front of the door Between the lines Along the path

ECHO
In the way it was in the street
it was in the back it was
in the house it was in the room
it was in the dark it was

FAT FATE
Be at That this
Come as If when
Stay or Soon then
Ever happen It will

LOOK
Particular pleasures weather measures or
Dimestore delights faced with such sights.

HERE
Outstretched innocence
Implacable distance
Lend me a hand
See if it reaches

TIME
Of right Of wrong Of up Of down
Of who Of how Of when Of one
Of then Of if Of in Of out
Of feel Of friend Of it Of now

MORAL
Now the inevitable
As in tales of woe
The inexorable toll
It takes, it takes.

EAT
Head on backwards
Face front neck's
Pivot bunched flesh
Drops jowled brunch.

TOFFEE
Little bit patted pulled
Stretched set let cool.

CASE
Whenas To for
If where From in
Past place Stated want
Gain granted Planned or

HAVE A HEART
Have heart Find head
Feel pattern Be wed
Smell water See sand
Oh boy Ain't life grand

OH OH
Now and then
Here and there
Everywhere
On and on

WINTER
Season's upon us
Weather alarms us
Snow riot peace
Leaves struck fist.

DUTY
Let little Linda allow litigation
Foster faith's fantasy famously
And answer all apt allegations
Handmake Harold's homework handsomely

GOTCHA
Passion's particulars
Steamy hands
Unwashed warmth
One night stands

WEST ACTON SUMMER
Cat's rats, Mother's brother
Vacation's patience, loud clouds
Fields far, seize trees
School's rules, friends tend
Lawn's form, barn's beams
Hay's daze, swallows follow
Sun's sunk, moon mends
Echo's ending, begin again

FAR
"Far be it from Harry to alter the sense of drama
inherent in the almighty tuxedo . . ."

"Far be it from Harry"
Sit next to Mary
See how the Other
Follows your Mother

PAT'S
Pat's place
Pattern's face
Aberrant fact
Changes that

FOUR'S
Four's forms
Back and forth
Feel way Hindside
Paper route Final chute

SENTENCES
Indefatigably alert when hit still hurt.
Whenever he significantly alters he falters.
Wondrous weather murmured mother.
Unforgettable twist in all such synthesis.
Impeccably particular you always were.
Laboriously enfeebled he still loved people.

WORDS
Driving to the expected
Place in mind in
Place of mind in
Driving to the expected

HERE
You have to reach
Out more it's
Farther away from
You it's here

DATA
Exoneration's face
Echoed distaste
Privileged repetition
Makeshift's decision—

.

Now and then
Behind time's
Emptied scene and
Memory's mistakes—

.

You are here
And there too
Being but one
Of you—

SCATTER
All that's left of coherence.

ECHO AGAIN
Statement keep talking
Train round bend over river into distance

DOOR
Everything's before you
were here.

SUMMER '38
Nubble's Light a sort
of bump I thought—
a round insistent
small place

not like this—
it was a bluff,
up on the edge
of the sea.

AIR
Lift up so you're
Floating out
Of your skin at
The edge but
Mostly up seeming
Free of the ground.

ECHOES
Think of the
Dance you could do
One legged man
Two legged woman.

THERE
Hard to be unaddressed—
Empty to reflection—
Take the road east—
Be where it is.

ECHOES
Sunrise always first—
That light—is it
Round the earth—what
Simple mindedness.

STAR
Where
It is
There
You are

.

Out there
In here
Now it is
Was also

.

Up where
It will be
And down
Again

.

No one
Point
To it
Ever

Echo

Brutish recall
seems useless now
to us all.

But my teeth you said
were yellow
have stayed nonetheless.

It was your handsomeness
went sour, your
girlish insouciance,

one said.
Was being afraid
neurotic?

Did you talk of it.
Was the high cliff jumpable.
Enough enough?

Fifty years
have passed.
I look back,

while you stand here,
see you there, still
see you there.

Thinking of Wallace Stevens

After so many years the familiar
seems even more strange, the hands

one was born with even more remote, the feet
worn to discordant abilities, face fainter.

I love, loved you, Esmeralda, darling Bill.
I liked the ambience of others, the clotted crowds.

Inside it was empty, at best a fountain in winter,
a sense of wasted, drab park, a battered nonentity.

Can I say the whole was my desire?
May I again reiterate my single purpose?

No one can know me better than myself,
whose almost ancient proximity grew soon tedious.

The joy was always to know it was the joy,
to make all acquiesce to one's preeminent premise.

The candle flickers in the quick, shifting wind.
It reads the weather wisely in the opened window.

So it is the dullness of mind one cannot live without,
this place returned to, this place that was never left.

A Note

I interrupt these poems to bring you some lately particular information,
which is that such coherence or determining purpose as I presumed my-
self to have in a collection such as this (not very long ago at all) seems
now absent. Thus I collect much as a magpie (in Duncan's engaging sense)
all that attracts me. Be it said once again that writing is a pleasure. So I

am not finally building roads or even thinking to persuade the reader of
some conviction I myself hold dear. I am trying to practice an art, which
has its own insistent authority and needs no other, however much it may,
in fact, say. I had not really understood what the lone boy whistling in
the graveyard was fact of. Now I listen more intently.

Alex's Art

Art's a peculiar division of labors—"a small town cat before he joined
    (the band"—
as if the whole seen world were then an echo

Of anyone's mind in a past tense of Arabs, say,
inventing tents in the early hours of meager history.

It is "an ever fixed mark," a parallel, "blue
suede persuasion," a thing out there beyond

Simple industries and all those sad captains thereof.
It is a place elsewhere, time enough, "please

Pass the bacon" again, oh finite, physical person.
Listen to the wonders of how it's been, or how it is

And will be, now as sky lifts the faint edge of morning in yellowish
    (grey tones,
as I hear nothing, as I listen again, brought into myself,

As all of it now tails back of me in flooded pockets,
as even the hum of the machine, call it, sings its persistent song—

As each so-called moment, each plunge and painful recovery
of breath echoes its precedent, its own so-called raison d'être,

Arch or meager, living or forgotten, here or finally there,
as it thinks the givens, feels around for place to put them down,

No metaphoric by-pass, no hands in pockets, no home alone,
no choice, nowhere to sit down. But what is immensely evident,

Even in each particular such as always that "where are the snows of
‹yesteryear,"
is why pay so painfully in advance for what can never be here now?

Look at it this way. You know those simple coordinates of A and B.
Add C, the comedian. Add X and Y. Add the apparent sun and simple sky.

Add everything and everyone you've ever known. Still empty? Still
only time enough to settle the bills, or try to, to be kind to the dog who
‹waits?

Trees' edges defined more now as sun lifts, lifted, to higher point in far
‹off space.
I see this world as a common picture, having among others two
‹dimensions

As well as a presently pleasant odor like, say, fresh cut hay. I hear little,
given my ears are not working quite properly, and I have gone indoors

A long, long way down a tunnel to where my TV sits on a table,
and I sit before it, watching the news. All a world in mind, isn't it,

As we do or do not get the bad guys? I don't know. But I still can see,
and I look at you. The simple question still. Can you see me?

Dutch Boy

I'd thought
boy caught stopped

dike's dripping water
with finger

put in hole
held it all back

oh hero
stayed steadfast

through night's black
sat waited

till dawn's light
when people came

repaired the leak
rescued

sad boy. But
now I see what

was the fact
he was stuck

not finger in hole was
but he could not

take it out
feared he'd be caught

be shamed
blamed

so sat
through the night

uncommonly distraught
in common fright.

Fragment

Slight you lift.
Edge skin down.
Circle seen.
Places now found.

Featured face.
Hand in when.
Disposition.
Distrust.

Three

Faint Faces

I can't move
as formerly but
still keep
at it as the

ground cants
rising to manage
some incumbent
cloud of

reference left
years back
the tracks absent
events it

was part of
parting and
leaving still
here still there.

Time

How long for the small yellow flowers
ride up from the grasses' bed,
seem patient in that place—

What's seen of all I see
for all I think of it—
but cannot wait, no, *cannot* wait.

The afternoon, a time, floats
round my head, a boat I float on,
sit on, sat on, still rehearse.

I seem the faded register, the misplaced camera,
the stuck, forgotten box, the unread book,
the rained on paper or the cat went out for good.

Nowhere I find it now or even
stable within the givens, thus comfortable to reason,
this sitting on a case, this fact sans face.

This House

Such familiar space
out there, the window
frame's locating

focus I could
walk holding
on to

through air from
here to there,
see it where

now fog's close
denseness floats
the hedgerow up

off apparent ground,
the crouched, faint
trees lifting up

from it, and more
close down
there in front

by roof's slope, down,
the stonewall's conjoining,
lax boulders sit,

years' comfortable pace
unreturned, placed
by deliberation and

limit make their
sprawled edge. Here
again inside

the world one thought of,
placed in this aged box
moved here from

family site
lost as us, time's
spinning confusions

are what
one holds on to.
Hold on, dear house,

'gainst the long hours
of emptiness, against
the wind's tearing force.

You are my mind
made particular
my heart in its place.

The Road

Whatever was else or less
or more or even
the sinister prospect
of nothing left,

not this was anticipated,
that there would be no one
even to speak of it.
Because all had passed over

to wherever they go.
Into the fiery furnace
to be burned to ash.
Into the ground,

into mouldering skin and bone
with mind the transient guest,
with the physical again dominant
in the dead flesh under the stones.

Was this the loved hand, the
mortal "hand still capable of grasping . . ."
Who could speak
to make death listen?

One grows older,
gets closer.
It's a long way home,
this last walking.

The Place

Afternoon it changes
and lifts, the heavy
fog's gone and the wind

rides the field, the flowers,
to the far edge
beyond what's seen.

It's a dream
of something or
somewhere I'd been

or would be, a place
I had made
with you, marked out

with string
years ago. Hannah
and Will are

no longer those
children
simply defined.

Is it weather
like wind blows, and all
to the restless sea?

Personal

"Urgent" what the message says.
First of all purposes.
The loss of place for porpoises.
Less use of detergents.

Lack luster linens.
Tables without chairs.
Passionate abilities given little leeway.
They never were.

Thirties a faded time.
Forties the chaos of combat.
Fifties lots of loneliness.
Sixties redemption.

I look at you.
You look at me.
We see.
We continue.

Parade

Measure's inherent
in the weight,
the substance itself
the person.

How far, how
long, how high,
what's there
now and why.

Cries in the dark,
screams out,
silence,
throat's stuck.

Fist's a weak grip,
ears blotted with echoes,
mind fails focus
and's lost.

Feet first,
feet last,
what difference,
down or up.

You were the shape
I took in the dark.
You the me
apprehended.

Wonders!
Simple fools,
rulers, all of us
die too.

On the way
much happiness
of a day,
no looking back.

Onward

"We cannot give you any support
if we don't know who you are."

You cannot drive on this road
if you do not have a car.

I cannot sleep at night
if I won't go to bed.

They used to be my friends
but now they are dead.

One Way

Oh I so
like the
avoidance
common

to patient
person stands
on curb waiting
to cross.

Why not run out
get clobbered truck
car or bus
busted

to bits
smiling even
in defeat
stay simple.

Such sizing up
of reality
whiff of reaction
you will not

walk far alone
already the crowd
is with you or else
right behind.

I see you
myself sit
down walk too
no different

just the patient
pace we keep
defeats us
in the street.

The Wordsworths

FOR WARREN

The Wordsworths afoot
fresh fields' look

birds hop on gravestone
small lake beyond

up long dank road
Coleridge's home—

Out this window I see
a man turning hay

early sun's edge
strike the green hedge

a blue round of field flower
mark the fresh hour

high spike of mullein
look over walled stone—

House slope blacked roof
catches eye's proof

returns me to day
passed far away

Dorothy took note,
William wrote.

Here

Seen right of head,
window's darkening outlook
to far field's slope
past green hedgerow.

Here, slanted lengthening
sun on back wall's
dancing shadows,
now comes night.

Five Variations on "Elation"

FOR BILL McCLUNG

This sudden
uplift elation's
pride's brought out!

Even ambiguity's
haughtily exalted oh
rushed, raised spirit.

    ·

Rushed unexpected my
heart leaps up when
I behold the sudden
as in the common.

    ·

Curiously with pride
above common lot to walk,

to be lifted up
and out, exalted.

    ·

His elation was brief?
Brought back to earth,

still for a time
it was otherwise.

    ·

Faded but unforgotten
if down once
uplifted if unsure
once proud if
inside once out.

    ·

ECHO
Elation's ghost
dance echoes
little, leaves no
traces, counts
no number—

Wants from no
one privilege. Has
no pride by being it.
If then recognized,
needs no company.

What wind's echo,
uplifted spirit?
Archaic feelings
flood the body.
Ah! accomplished.

Edges

FOR PEN'S BIRTHDAY (EVERYDAY)

Edges of the field, the blue flowers, the reddish wash of
the grasses, the cut green path up to the garden
plot overgrown with seedlings and weeds—

green first of all, but light, the cut of the sunlight
edges each shift of the vivid particulars, grown large
—even the stones large in their givens, the shadows massing

their bulk, and so seeing I could follow out to another
edge of the farther field, where trees are thick on the sky's
edge, thinking I am not simply a response to this, this light,

not just an agency sees and vaguely adumbrates, adds an opinion.
There is no opinion for life, no word more or less general.
I had begun and returned, again and again, to find you finally,

felt it all gather, as here, to be a place again, and wanted to
shuck the husk of habits, to lift myself to you in this sunlight.
If it is age, then what does age matter? If it is older or younger,

what moment notes it? In this containment there cannot
be another place or time. It all lives by its being
here and now, this persistent pleasure, ache of promise, misery of all
       ‹that's lost.

Now as if this moment had somehow secured to itself a body,
had become you, just here and now, the wonders inseparable
in this sunlight, *here,* had come to me again.

Billboards

AGE
Walking on
the same
feet
birth

provided,
I is not
the simple
question

after all,
nor *you*
an interesting
answer.

MORAL
Practice
your humility
elsewhere
'cause it's just another

excuse for privilege,
another place not
another's, another
way you get to get.

BIG TIME
What you got
to kill now isn't
dead enough
already? Wait,

brother, it *dies,* it
no way can *live*
without you, it's
waiting in line.

ECHO
It was a thoughtful
sense of paced
consideration,
whatever the agenda

had prompted as
subject. "Here we
are," for example, or
"There they were" . . .

So all together now,
a deep breath, a
fond farewell.
Over.

TRUE OR FALSE
"One little
freckle
houses
bacteria

equal
to the population
of New York—"
You cannot

breathe, scratch
or move
sans killing
what so

lives on you.
There are
no vacancies, no
rooms with a view.

DREAM
What's the truth
for except it
makes a place for
common entrances, an

old way home down
the street 'midst faces,
the sounds' flooding
poignance, the approach?

Sky

Now that the weather softens the
end of winter in the tips of
trees' buds grow lighter a yellow
air of lifting slight but persistent
warmth you walk past the street's
far corner with turbanlike color swathed
hat and broad multicolored shawl hangs
down over your trunklike blue cloth
coat with legs black dog's tugging
pull on leash's long cord I walk quickly
to catch up to you pulled equally by
your securing amplitude, blue love!

A Book

FOR PAM AND LEW

A book of such
sweetness the
world attends
one after

another a found
explicit fondness
mends the tear
threads intercross

here where there
repairs a cluster
comes mitigates
irritation reads words.

A View at Evening

Cut neat path out
to darkening
garden plot
old field's forgot.

Far hedge row's
growth goes
down the hill
where blurred

trees depend,
find an end
in distance
under dark clouds.

The upright space,
place, fades sight,
sees echoes,
green, green, green.

This Room

Each thing given
place in the pattern
rather find
place in mind

a diverse face
absent past
shelf of habits
bits pieces

eye lost then
love's mistakes
aunt's battered house
off foundation

children's recollection
tokens
look back
chipped broken

room goes on
dark winter's edge
now full with sun
pales the worn rug.

Sins

A hand's part,
mouth's open look,
foot beside
the long leg.

Away again.
Inside the house
open windows
look out.

It was fun.
Then it's gone.
Come again
some time.

Time's Fixed

Time's fixed
as ticking instrument,
else day's insistent
ending into

which one walks,
finds the door shut,
and once again
gets caught, gets caught.

A captive heart,
a head, a hand,
an ear, the empty bed
is here—

A dull, an
unresponding man
or woman dead
to plan or plot.

Between what was
and what might be
still seems to be
a life.

Heaven

Wherever they've
gone they're
not here
anymore

and all
they stood
for is empty
also.

Echoes

In which the moment
just left reappears or
seems as if present
again its fact intact—

In which a willing
suspension of disbelief
alters not only the judgment
but all else equally—

In which the time passes
vertically goes up and
up to a higher place a
plane of singular clarity—

In which these painfully small
endings shreds of emptying
presence sheddings of seeming
person can at last be admitted.

Echo

It was never
simple to wait,
to sit quiet.

Was there still
another way round,
a distance to go —

as if an echo
hung in
the air before

one was heard,
before a word
had been said.

What was love
and where
and how did one get there.

Echo

The return of things
round the great
looping bend in the road

where you remember
stood in mind
greyed encumbrances

patient dead dog
long lost love
till chair's rocking

became roar
sitting static
end of vision

day seems held up
by white hands were
looking for what was

gone couldn't come
back what was with
it wouldn't come looking.

Echo

FOR ECK

Find your way out
no doubt
or in
again begin

Spaces wait
faced
in the dark
no waste

Were there
was here
was
always near

Sit down to see
be quiet be
friend
the end

Valentine

FOR PEN

Home's still heart
light in the window
all the familiar
tokens of patience

moved finally out
to let place be
real as it can be
people people

all as they are
and pasteboard red heart
sits there on table
inside the thump bump

passing thought
practical meat
slur and slurp
contracting lump

all for you
wanting a meaning
without you
it would stop

Coda
ROMAN SKETCHBOOK

Roman Sketchbook

AS
As you come and go
from a place you sense
the way it might seem
to one truly there as
these clearly determined persons
move on the complex spaces

and hurry to their obvious
or so seeming to you
destinations. "Home," you think,
"is a place still there for all,"
yet now you cannot
simply think it was

or can be the same. It
starts with a small
dislocating ache, the foot
had not been that problem,
but you move nonetheless
and cannot remember the word

for foot, *fuss, pied?* some
thing, a childhood pleasure
she said she could put her
foot in her mouth but
that way is the past again
someone's, the greying air

looks like evening here, the
traffic moves so densely,
you push close to the walls
of the buildings, the stinking
cars, bikes, people push by.
No fun in being one here,

you have to think. You must
have packed home in mind,
made it up, and yet all
people wait there, still patient
if distracted by what happens.
Out in the night the lights

go on, the shower has cleared the air.
You have a few steps more to the door.
You see it open as you come up, triggered
by its automatic mechanism, a greeting
of sorts, but no one would think of that.
You come in, you walk to the room.

IN THE CIRCLE
In the circle of an
increased limit all
abstracted felt event now

entered at increasing distance
ears hear faintly eye sees
the fading prospects and in-

telligence unable to get the
name back fails and posits
the blank. It largely moves

as a context, habit of being
here as *there* approaches, and
one pulls oneself in to prepare

for the anticipated slight shock—
boat bumping the dock, key
turning in lock, the ticking clock?

APOSTROPHE
Imaginal sharp distances we
push out from, confident
travelers, whose worlds are
specific to bodies— Realms of
patient existence carried without
thought come to unexpected end
here where nothing waits.

HERE
Back a street is the sunken
pit of the erstwhile market
first century where the feral

cats now wait for something
to fall in and along the
far side is the place where

you get the bus, a broad
street divided by two
areas for standing with a

covered provision, etc. *Antichi!*
Zukofsky'd say—all of it
humbling age, the pitted, pitiful

busts someone's sprayed with blue
paint, the small streets laboring
with compacted traffic, the generous

dank stink floods the evening air.
Where can we go we will not
return to? Each moment, somewhere.

READING / RUSSELL SAYS, "THERE IS NO RHINOCEROS IN THIS ROOM"
Wittgenstein's insistence to Russell's
equally asserted context of world as
experienced *things* was it's *propositions*
we live in and no "rhinoceros" can
proceed other than fact of what so states
it despite you look under tables or chairs
and open all thinking to prove there's
no rhinoceros here when you've
just brought it in on a plate
of proposed habituated *meaning*
by opening your mouth and out it pops.

ELEVEN AM
Passionate increase of particulars
failing passage to outside formulae
of permitted significance who cry
with foreign eyes out there the
world of all others sky and sun
sudden rain washes the window
air fresh breeze lifts the heavy
curtain to let the room out into
place the street again and people.

IN THE ROOMS
In the rooms of building James
had used in "Portrait
of a Lady" looking up to
see the frescoes and edging
of baroque seeming ornament
as down on the floor we are

still thinking amid the stacks
of old books and papers, racks,
piles, aisles of patient quiet
again in long, narrow,
pewlike seated halls for
talking sit and think of it.

HOW LONG
How long
to be here
wherever
it is—

I THINK
I think
the steps up
to the flat
parklike top

of hill by the Quirinale look
like where I'd walked when
last here had stopped
before I'd gone in

down to the Coliseum's
huge bulk
the massed rock
and the grassed plot

where the Christians fought
and traffic roars round
as if time
only were mind

or all this
was reminiscence
and what's real
is not.

ROOM
World's become shrunk to
square space high ceiling
box with washed green
sides and mirror the eye
faces to looks to see the
brown haired bent head
red shirt and moving pen
top has place still apparent
whatever else is or was.

OUTSIDE
That curious arrowed sound up
from plazalike street's below
window sun comes in through
small space in vast green drapes
opened for the air and sounds
as one small person's piercing cry.

WALK
Walk out now as if
to the commandment
go forth or is it
come forth "Come out
with your hands up . . ."
acquiescent to each step.

WATCHING
Why didn't I call to the
two tense people passing us
sitting at edge of plaza
whom I knew and had reason
to greet but sat watching them
go by with intent nervous faces the
rain just starting as they
went on while I sat with another
friend under large provided umbrella
finishing dregs of the coffee, watching?

VILLA CELIMONTANA
As we walk past crumbling
walls friend's recalling his
first love an American
girl on tour who then
stays for three months in
Rome with him then off
for home and when he
finally gets himself to
New York two years or more
later they go out in
company with her friend
to some place on Broadway
where McCoy Tyner's playing
and now half-loaded comfortable
the friend asks, "What part of
yourself do you express
when you speak English?"
Still thinking of it and me now
as well with *lire* circling my head.

THE STREET
All the various
members of the Italian
Parliament walking
past my lunch!

AS WITH
As with all such
the prospect of ending
gathers now friends take
leave and the afternoon
moves toward the end
of the day. So too mind
moves forward to its place
in time and *now,* one
says, *and now* —

OBJECT
The expandable enveloping flat flesh
he pulls in to center in hotel
room's safety like taking in
the wash which had flapped
all day in the wind. *In,* he
measures his stomach, *in* like
manner his mind, *in*side his
persistent discretion, way, *un-*
opened to anything by *im*pression . . .

· · ·

So often in such Romantic apprehension
he had wanted only to roam
but howsoever he weighed it or waited
whatsoever was "Rome" was home.

Life & Death

One

Histoire de Florida

You're there
still behind
the mirror,
brother face.

Only yesterday
you were younger,
now you
look old.

Come out
while there's still time
left
to play.

.

Waking, think of sun through
compacted tree branches,
the dense
persistent light.

Think of heaven,
home,
a heart of gold,
old song of friend's

dear love and all
the faint world it
reaches to,
it wants.

.

Out over that piece of water
where the sound is, the place
it loops round on the map from
the frontal ocean and makes a
spit of land this sits on, here, flat,
filled with a patent detritus left
from times previous whatever
else was here before become
now brushy conclave thick with
hidden birds, nimble, small lizards.

.

Whatever, whatever.
Wherever, what-
ever, whenever— It won't
be here anymore—
What one supposes
dead is, but what a simple ending,
pain, fear, unendurable
wrenched division, breakdown
of presumed function, truck's broken
down again, no one left
to think of it, fix it, walk on.
Will one fly away on angel wings,
rise like a feather, lift
in the thin air— But again returned,
preoccupied, he counts his life
like cash in emptying pockets.
Somebody better help him.

.

Remember German artist
(surely "conceptual" or
"happenings") ate himself,
cut bits from his body
on stage while audience
watched, it went well
for awhile. But then
he did something wrong
and bled to death.
The art is long
to learn, life short.

.

It must be anecdotal,
sudden sights along the so-called way,
Bunting's advice that David Jones
when he first met him had moved but once
in adult life and then only
when the building burned down
to a place across the street.
They were having tea
when abruptly Jones got up,
went to an easel at the far end of the room
whereon a sheet of drawing paper
with, in his immaculate script, a 't,'
added an 'h' to say,
"I'll have the 'e' by Monday!"
Affections flood me,
love lights light in like eyes . . .

.

Your two eyes will me
suddenly slay . . .
Such echoes
of heaven on earth

in mind as if
such *a glass* through which
seen *darkly*
such reflected truth.

What words, then,
if you love me,
what *beauty*
not to be *sustained*

will separate
finally
dancer
from *dance.*

        .

Sun meantime
shining

just now (now) a
yellow slid

oblong
patch (light)

from wide
window

        .

But don't get physical
with me. Topper, or the Cheshire cat
whose head could appear grinning
in the tree. Could appear
in the window.
Could see
in the dark.

.

You still think
death is a subject,
or a place
in time?

Like halving the distance,
the arrow that never gets there.
I died and came back again
to the very spot I'd seemingly

left from, in a Raj-like hotel,
Calcutta, 1944. From lunch of prawns
got up and went to my room,
an hour later dimly recall was on hands and knees

crawling to quondam toilet
to vomit and shit, then must
have collapsed completely en route back
to the bed and a long time later heard

voice (hotel doctor's, they told me)
saying, must get him to hospital,
he can't die here. But I'd gone away
down long faint space of path

or up, or simply out,
was moving away into a reassuring distance
of somewhere
(heaven? I don't think so —

My temperature was 96 etc.
Délires! Whatever— Wherever
had come to, gone to,
I wasn't there.

.

Leary at Naropa for celebration
of Kerouac I remember saying, it's dumb to die—
It's for squares! Gregory
thought it a dumb thing to say to the young.

Was it metaphysical?
Did he mean something else.
Whether with drugs or not,
be rid of such terminal dependence?

As if, and why not,
closure were just fact
of a clogged pipe,
all coming to naught?

Get it out.
Open up?
—But the syntax would be,
"What proceeds and what follows,"

in Pound's phrase,
like a river,
the emptying sounds
of paradise.

.

In pajamas still
late morning sun's at my back
again through the window,
figuring mind still, figuring place
I am in, which is me,
solipsistic, a loop yet moving, moving,
with these insistent proposals
of who, where, when,
what's out there, what's in,
what's the so-called art of anything,
hat, house, hand, head, heart, and so on,
quickly banal. Always reflections.
No light on the water, no clouds lifting, bird's flap taking off—
Put the food in mouth, feel throat swallowing,
warmth is enough.

Emotions recollected in tranquillity . . .
which is what?
Feelings now are not quiet, daughter's threatened
kidneys, sister's metal knee replacement, son's
vulnerable neighborhood friendships, Penelope's social
suitors, whom I envy, envy.
Age. Age.
Locked in my mind,
my body, toes broken, skin
wrinkling up, look to the ceiling
where, through portals of skylight,
two rectangular glass boxes in the stained wood,
the yellow light comes, an outside is evident.
There is no irony, no patience.

There is nothing to wait for
that isn't here, and it will happen.
Happiness is thus lucky.
Not I but the wind that blows through me.

.

Another day. Drove to beach,
parked the car on the edge of the road
and walked up on the wooden ramp provided,
then stopped just before the steps down to the sand
and looked out at the long edge of the surf, the sun glitter,
the backdrop of various condominiums and cottages,
the usual collective of people, cars, dogs and birds.
It was sweet to see company,
and I was included.

Yet Crusoe—
Whose mind was that, Defoe's?
Like Kafka's *Amerika,* or Tom Jones come to London.
Or Rousseau, or Odysseus—
One practices survival
much as we did when kids and would head for the woods
with whatever we could pilfer or elders gave us,
doughnuts, cookies, bread—
Even in one's own terror,
one is proud of a securing skill.

But what so turned things
to pain, and if Mandelstam's poem is found scratched
on cell wall in the gulag
by anonymous hand,
and that's all of either we know—

Why isn't that instance of the same
side of world Robinson Crusoe comes to,
footprint on sand a terror,
person finally discovered an adversary
he calls "Friday,"
who then he learns "to be good"—

But I wouldn't, I can't
now know or resolve
when it all became so singular,
when first that other door closed,
and the beach and the sunlight faded,
surf's sounds grew faint, and one's thoughts took over,
bringing one home.

.

At a dinner
in Kuala Lumpur

where I was the guest
together with a sewerage expert

had most recently worked in Saudi Arabia
where drainage was the problem,

and here it was the same,
we talked of conveniences,

shopping malls, suburbs,
and what had been hauled over

from stateside habit,
the bars and people,

while just down the street
was what the Kuala Lumpurians called

The Backside of Hell,
a short alley of small doorways

and open stalls.
They said here anything was possible.

Meantime in our hotel lobby
they had dyed some chicks a weird bluish pink

and put them in a little cage
out front for Easter.

It's always one world
if you can get there.

·

HISTOIRE DE FLORIDA
Old persons swinging their canted metal detectors,
beach's either end out of sight beyond the cement block highrises,
occasional cars drifting by in the lanes provided,
sheer banks of the dunes bulkheaded by bulldozers,
there a few cars backed up, parked.
People walk by or stretch out on cots,
turning in the sun's heat, tanning.

The line of the surf at some distance, small,
the white edge of breakers where the surfers cluster.
On the far horizon, east, is bulk of a freighter,
to the north, tower of a lighthouse across the inlet.
Back of it all the town sells the early tourists,
the stores filling with elderly consumers.
The old are gathering for an old-time ritual.

One knows that in the waters hereabouts, in a particular spring,
Ponce de Leon staggered in so as *to live forever.*
But poisoned with infection from a local's arrow
and conned by the legend of eternal youth,
he'd led all his people into a bloody cul-de-sac
and ended himself being fed to alligators
ate him skin and bones, leaving no trace.

So it may be we all now look
for where the first of these old folks went down,
seeing his own face in the placid creek,
hearing the far-off murmur of the surf,
feeling his body open in the dark,
the warmth of the air, the odor of the flowers,
the eternal maiden waiting soft in her bower.

.

This is the lovely time
of late afternoon
when the sun comes in
through slatted blinds.

The large glass panes
show streaks in the dust.
Bushy laurel's green leaves
turn golden beyond.

I hear plane pass over
high in the sky,
see flowers in vase tremble
with table's movement.

Company's become
room's quiet hum.
This hanging silence
fills with sound.

.

Determined reading
keeps the mind's attention
off other things, fills
the hole in symbolic stocking

now that Xmas approaches —
a truck through proverbial night,
the buzzes, roars, of silence
I hear here

all alone.
Poor, wee Robbie!
Flickering light in small window,
meager head and heart in hand,

I recall William Bartram
somewhere in 18th century Florida
on night not unlike this one,
after he'd hauled his skiff up on shore,

then laid down, so he wrote,
to sleep when sudden uproar,
thumpings, bangings, poundings!
all seeming very close,

awakened him to possibility
he was going to die.
But, stalwart,
checked it out

to find an alligator had clambered up
and over the gunnels of his boat
to get dead fish Bartram had left inside —
and all was finally well.

He drew great pictures of "the natives,"
looking like quaint
18th century English persons
in beguiling states of undress.

He had a heart I wish I had.
My car is parked in the driveway.
My door is locked. I do not want
to go outside.

    .

What was resistance.
How come to this.
Wasn't body's package
obvious limit,

could I fly,
could I settle,
could I even
be I . . .

And for what want,
watching man die
on tv in Holland, wife
sitting by.

She said, "He's
going off alone
for the first time
in our lives."

He told her,
"to the stars, to the
Milky Way,"
relaxed, and was gone.

What is Florida
to me or me
to Florida except
so defined.

    .

You've left a lot out
Being in doubt
you left
it out

Your mother
Aunt Bernice
in Nokomis
to the west

and south (?)
in trailer park
Dead now for years
as one says

You've left
them out
David
your son

Your friend
John
You've left
them out

You thought
you were writing
about
what you felt

You've left it out
Your love
your life
your home

your wife
You've
left her
out

No one is one
No one's alone
No world's that small
No life

You left it out

.

The shell was the apparent
inclusion, that *another* might be here.
Form, the provision,
what one took, or didn't,

from another. What form
did it take,
what way
did it matter?

My mind was a supermarket
or a fading neighborhood store.
I couldn't find anything anymore,
or just didn't have it.

I is another . . .
and another, another,
blocks fading, streets
fading, into an emptying distance.

Who tore it down.
Where was it, what
was it. Where do you think
you left it?

My mother in Nokomis,
Aunt Bernice in Nokomis,
David in Sarasota,
Mary Ann, Cecelia, Rebecca

in Sarasota, John in
Sarasota, or Long Island,
Pen, Will and Hannah,
Helen, in Buffalo—

how use *them* simply as loci,
points of reference,
who made me substance?
Sarah calls to say she is pregnant

and *that* is a delicious sound—
like the music Caliban hears
sometimes in Prospero's cell
surrounding him.

·

Rise into the air and look down
and see it there, the pendant form of it,
the way it goes out, alone, into an ocean,

the end of a pattern suddenly extended
to cover, in itself, the western reach, the gulf close beyond.
Its fragile surfaces are watery, swamps to the south,

to the north where its population gathers in flat cities,
sandy wastes, oaks, palmetto, laurel, pine and (for me)
an unidentified particularity more seen, felt, than known.

Perhaps the whole place is a giant pier out
into nothing, or into all that is other, all else.
Miles and miles of space are here in unexpected senses,

sky washed with clouds, changing light, long sunsets
sinking across water and land, air that freshens, intimate.
Endless things growing, all horizontal, an edge, a rise only of feet

above the sea's surface, or the lakes, the ponds, the rivers,
all out, nothing that isn't vulnerable, no depths, no rooted senses
other than the actual fabric of roots, skin of survivals.

.

I placed a jar in Tennessee,
In Florida I placed a jar
And round it was, upon a hill . . .
And all around it grew important air

. . . And tall and of a port in air.
It was my first time there
It took dominion everywhere.
and I was far from home and scared

The jar was gray and bare.
in Florida, like nothing else
. . . Like nothing else in Tennessee.
In Florida. Like nothing else.

Two
OLD POEMS, ETC.

Echo

of the nameless
breather" — The brother,
sister, of the faceless
now adamant body, all
still unsaid, unfledged,
unrecognized until
death all so sudden
comes for the people
and we are one
in this covenant, all the nameless,
those still breathing,
all brothers, sisters,
mothers, fathers,
just a piece of the real,
the fading action, one after one
this indifferent, inexorable, *bitter*
affliction strikes down—

Credo

Creo que si . . . I believe
it will rain
tomorrow . . . I believe
the son of a bitch

is going into the river . . .
I believe *All men are
created equal* —By your
leave a leafy

shelter over the exposed
person— *I'm a
believer* creature
of habit but without

out there a void of
pattern older
older the broken
pieces no longer

salvageable bits
but incommensurate
chips yet must
get it back together.

*In God we
trust* emptiness privilege
will not not *perish*
perish *from this earth*—

In particular echo
of inside pushes
at edges all these years
collapse in slow motion.

The will to believe,
the will to be good,
the will to want
a way out—

Humanness, like
you, man. Us—pun
for once beyond reflective
mirror of brightening prospect?

I believe what it was
was a hope it could be
somehow what it was
and would so continue.

A plank to walk out on,
fair enough. *Jump!* said the pirate.
Believe me if all
those endearing young charms . . .

Here, as opposed to there,
even in confusions there seems
still a comfort,
still a faith.

I'd as lief
not leave, not
go away, not
not believe.

I believe in belief . . .
All said, whatever I can think of
comes from there,
goes there.

As it gets now impossible
to say, it's your hand
I hold to, still
your hand.

A Feeling

However far
I'd gone,
it was still
where it had all begun.

What stayed
was a feeling of difference,
the imagination
of adamant distance.

Some time,
place,
some other way it was,
the turned face

one loved,
remembered,
had looked for
wherever,

it was all now
outside
and in
was oneself again

except there too
seemed nowhere,
no air,
nothing left clear.

Silence

I can't speak so
simply of whatever
was then
the fashion

of silence
everyone's— Blue
expansive morning
and in

the lilac bush just
under window
farm house
spaces all

the teeming chatter
of innumerable birds—
I'd lie quiet
trying

to go to sleep late
evenings in summer
such buzzes settling
twitters

of birds— The relatives
in rooms underneath
me murmuring—
Listened hard to catch

faint edges of sounds
through blurs of a fading
spectrum now out
there forever.

Old Story

Like kid on float
of ice block sinking
in pond the field had made
from winter's melting snow

so wisdom accumulated
to disintegrate
in conduits of brain
in neural circuits faded

while gloomy muscles shrank
mind padded the paths
its thought had wrought
its habits had created

till like kid afloat
on ice block broken
on or inside the thing it stood
or was forsaken.

Given

Can you recall
distances, odors,
how far from the one
to the other, stalls

for the cows,
the hummocks one jumped to,
the lawn's webs,
touch, taste of specific

doughnuts, cookies,
what a pimple was
and all such way
one's skin was a place—

Touch, term, turn of curious fate.
Who can throw a ball,
who draw a face,
who knows how.

The Mirror

Seeing is believing.
Whatever was thought or said,

these persistent, inexorable deaths
make faith as such absent,

our humanness a question,
a disgust for what we are.

Whatever the hope,
here it is lost.

Because we coveted our difference,
here is the cost.

Pictures

The little bed
they put me in
with the grim pictures
facing in

The freak of death
for one so young
The fear of cuts
blood leaking out

The sudden abandon
of pleasure, summer
The seasons
The friends

One fall evening driving
in car with teacher
fellow student girl
sitting beside me

on way back from
first play seen
in Boston "Macbeth"
Why did they kill them

Why was my body
flooded
with tension
my small cock stiff

Loops

The other who I'd be
never the same as me
no way to step outside and see
more than some penitence of memory—

As day fades to the dust-filled light
in the window in the back wall beyond sight
where I can feel the coming night
like an old friend who sets all to rights—

In the constrictions of this determined scribble
despite slipping thought's wobble
the painful echoing senses of trouble
I've caused others and cannot end now—

Boxed in a life too late to know other
if there was ever any other
but fact of a lost tether
kept the other still somehow there—

To try now to say goodbye
as if one could try to die
in some peculiar mind
wanted to step outside itself for a last try—

To be oneself once and for all
to look through the window and see the wall
and want no more
of anything at all beyond.

Thinking

Grandmother I'd thought
to have called all together
night before dying
in the bed at the stairs' top

when I'd walked
with blackened sky
overhead the storm
and the lightning flashing

back past the Montagues
from the ice pond
and rotting icehouse
held the common pigeons

wanting all to go forward as ever
with grandmother
confidently ill I thought
giving last orders to us all

my mother the elder,
thus to take care
of sister Bernice and younger brother—
did she say as I thought,

I'm tired now
and roll over—
Was it book I'd read
said death's so determined—

whilst grandma crying
out to us
to come and help her
shook, coughed and died?

Goodbye

Now I recognize
it was always me
like a camera
set to expose

itself to a picture
or a pipe
through which the water
might run

or a chicken
dead for dinner
or a plan
inside the head

of a dead man.
Nothing so wrong
when one considered
how it all began.

It was Zukofsky's
*Born very young into a world
already very old . . .*
The century was well along

when I came in
and now that it's ending,
I realize it won't
be long.

But couldn't it all have been
a little nicer,
as my mother'd say. Did it
have to kill everything in sight,

did right always have to be so wrong?
I know this body is impatient.
I know I constitute only a meager voice and mind.
Yet I loved, I love.

I want no sentimentality.
I want no more than home.

"Present (Present) . . ."

"What is Williams' (Raymond's) tome . . ."
Where have all the flowers gone?

I put them right here on the table . . .
No one's been here but for Mabel.

God, my mind is slipping cogs,
gaps of pattern, mucho fog . . .

Yet I know whatever I
can ever think of ere I die,

'twill be in my head alone
that the symbiotic blur has formed—

to make no "we" unless "they" tell "us"
"you" is "me" and "I" is nameless.

"Tom" is wrong? "I" is right?
Is this the point at which "we" fight?

Us was never happy we,
all that's ever left is me.

Past is what I can't forget,
where the flowers got to yet—

Mabel's face, my mother's hands,
clouds o'erhead last year at Cannes,

Kenneth Koch's reaction when
we told him once at 3 AM

he should marry Barbara Epstein,
loosen up and have some fun.

"I remember. I remember—"
Memory, the great pretender,

says it happened, thinks it was,
this way, that way, just because

it was in my head today . . .
Present (present) passed away.

Help

Who said you didn't want
to keep what you've got
and would help the other guy
share the bulging pot

of goodies you got
just by being bought
on time by the plot
wouldn't give you a dime

sick or not
you've got to stay well
if you want to buy time
for a piece of the lot

where you all can hang out
when you aren't sick in bed
blood running out
bones broken down

eyes going blind
ears stuffed up
stomach a bloat
you battered old goat

but nothing to keep up
no payments to make
no insurance is fine
when you plan to die

when you don't mind the wait
if you can't stand up
and all the others are busy
still making money.

A Valentine for Pen

I love you, says the clock, paradoxically silent, watching
through the night with red eyes. *I love you,* says the long
wooden table across from the wide bed with the bookcase
upright beside it, the black lamp arching over, the old computer
waiting for its work. *I love you, I love you,* the echoes, reaches
of the tall room, the hanging pictures, the catalogs, clothes, the
cats securely sleeping on the disheveled old couch, the pulled up
small rug put over its cushions, all say it, the enclosing dear room,
the balcony above which opens at each end to bedrooms of the
children, *I love you,* says Hannah's ample particular heart, says
Will's wide responsive heart, says each resonance of every sweet
morning's opening, here said, again and again, *I love you.*

Breath

FOR SUSAN ROTHENBERG

Breath as a braid, a tugging
squared circle, "steam, vapour—
an odorous exhalation,"
breaks the heart when it
stops. It is the living, the
moment, sound's curious
complement to *breadth,*
brethren, "akin to BREED . . ."
And what see, feel, know as
"the air inhaled and exhaled
in respiration," in substantial
particulars—as a horse?

.

Not language paints,
pants, patient, a pattern.
A horse (here *horses*) is
seen. Archaic in fact,
the word alone
presumes a world,
comes willy-nilly thus back
to where it had all begun.
These horses *are,* they reflect
on us, their seeming ease
a gift to all that lives,
and looks and breathes.

Four Days in Vermont

Window's tree trunk's predominant face
a single eye-leveled hole where limb's torn off
another larger contorts to swell growing in around
imploding wound beside a clutch of thin twigs
hold to one two three four five six dry twisted
yellowish brown leaves flat against the other
grey trees in back stick upright then the glimpse
of lighter still greyish sky behind the close
welted solid large trunk with clumps of grey-green
lichen seen in boxed glass squared window back
of two shaded lamps on brown chiffonier between
two beds echo in mirror on far wall of small room.

·

(FOR MAGGIE)

Most, death left a hole
a place where she'd been
An emptiness stays
no matter what or who
No law of account not
There but for the
grace of God go I
Pain simply of want
last empty goodbye
Put hand on her head
good dog, good dog
feel her gone.

·

Tree adamant looks in
its own skin mottled with growths
its stubborn limbs
stick upright parallel
wanting to begin again
looking for sun in the sky
for a warmer wind
to walk off pull up
roots and move
to Boston be a table
a chair a house
a use a final fire.

.

What is truth *firm (as a tree)*
Your faith your trust your loyalty
Agrees with the facts makes
world consistent plights a troth
is friendly sits in the common term
All down the years all seasons all sounds
all persons saying things conforms confirms
Contrasts with "war equals confusion" *(worse)*
But *Dichtung und Wahrheit?* "Wahr-" is
very ("Verily I say unto you . . .") A compact now
Tree lights with the morning though *truth* be an oak
This is a maple, is a *tree*, as a very truth firm.

.

Do I rootless shift
call on the phone
daughter's warm voice
her mother's clear place
Is there wonder here
has it all gone inside

myself become subject
weather surrounds
Do I dare go out
be myself specific
be as the tree
seems to look in.

.

Breeze at the window
lifts the light curtains
Through the dark a light
across the faint space
Warmth out of season
fresh wash of ground
out there beyond
sits here waiting
For whatever time comes
herein welcome
Wants still
truth of the matter.

.

Neighbor's light's still on
outside above stoop
Sky's patchy breaks
of cloud and light
Around is a valley
over the hill
to the wide flat river
the low mountains secure
Who comes here with you
sits down in the room
what have you left
what's now to do.

.

Soon going day wanders on
and still tree's out there waiting
patient in time like a river and
truth a simple apple reddened
by frost and sun is found
where one had left it in time's company
No one's absent in mind None gone
Tell me the *truth* I want to say
Tell me all you know Will we live
or die As if the world were apart
and whatever tree seen were only here apparent
Answers, live and die. Believe.

The Dogs of Auckland

1
Curious, coming again here,
where I hadn't known where I was ever,

following lead of provident strangers,
around the corners, out to the edges,

never really looking back but kept
adamant forward disposition, a Christian

self-evident resolve, small balloon of purpose
across the wide ocean, friends, relations,

all left behind. Each day the sun rose, then set.
It must be the way life is, like they say, a story

someone might have told me. I'd have listened.
Like the story Murray recalled by Janet Frame

in which a person thinks to determine what's most necessary
to life, and strips away legs, arms, trunk —

to be left with a head, more specifically, a brain,
puts it on the table, and a cleaning woman comes in,

sees the mess and throws it into the dustbin.
Don't think of it, just remember? Just then there was a gorgeous

light on the street there, where I was standing, waiting
for the #005 bus at the end of Queen Street, just there on Customs,

West – dazzling sun, through rain. "George is/gorgeous/
George is . . ." So it begins.

2
Almost twenty years ago I fled my apparent life, went off
into the vast Pacific, though it was only miles and miles

in a plane, came down in Auckland Airport, was met by Russell Haley –
and he's still here with Jean, though they've moved

to the east coast a few hours away, and Alan Loney is here
as ever my friend. And Wystan, whose light I might see there

across the bay, blinking. And Alistair Paterson is here with a thirty-
four-foot boat up the harbor – as in comes the crew of *Black Magic*

with the America's Cup, in their yellow slickers, the cars moving down
Queen Street, the crowd there waiting some half million –

in the same dazzling light in which I see tiny, seemingly dancing
‹figures
at the roof's edge of the large building back of the square, looking
‹down.

How to stay real in such echoes? How be, finally, anywhere the body's
‹got to?
You were with friends, sir? Do you know their address . . .

They walk so fast through Albert Park. Is it my heart causes these
awkward, gasping convulsions? I can mask the grimace with a smile,

can match the grimace with a smile. I can. *I think I can.*
Flooded with flat, unyielding sun, the winter beds of small plants

form a pattern, if one looks, a design. There is Queen Victoria still,
and not far from her the statue of a man. Sit down, sit down.

3 *(for Pen)*

Scale's intimate. From the frame and panes of the fresh white
painted windows in the door, to the deck, second floor, with its

white posts and securing lattice of bars, but nothing, *nothing* that
would ever look like that, just a small porch, below's the garden,

winter sodden, trampoline, dark wet green pad pulled tight, a lemon
tree thick with fruit. And fences, backyards, neighbors surrounding, in

all the sloping, flattened valley with trees stuck in like a kid's picture,
palms, Norfolk pine, stubby ones I can't name, a church spire, brownish

red at the edge of the far hill, also another prominent bald small dome,
both of which catch the late sun and glow there near the head of
      ‹Ponsonby Road.

The Yellow Bus stops up the street, where Wharf comes into Jervois Road,
off Buller to Bayfield, where we are. I am writing this, sitting at the table,

and love you more and more. When you hadn't yet got here, I set to
      ‹each morning
to learn "New Zealand" (I thought) as if it were a book simply. I listened
      ‹to everyone.

Now we go to bed as all, first Will and Hannah, in this rented house,
      ‹then us,
lie side by side, reading. Then off with the light and to sleep, to slide
      ‹close up

to one another, sometimes your bottom tucked tight against my belly or
mine lodged snug in your lap. *Sweet dreams, dear heart, till the*
      ‹*morning comes.*

4

Back again, still new, from the south
where it's cold now, and people didn't seem to

know what to do, cars sliding, roads blocked with snow,
walk along here through the freshening morning

down the wet street past green plastic garbage bins,
past persistent small flowering bushes, trees. Like the newcomer

come to town, the dogs bark and one on a porch
across from the house where we live makes a fuss

when I turn to go in through the gate. Its young slight
mistress comes out as if in dream, scolds the sad dog,

cuffing it with shadowy hands, then goes back in.
I wonder where sounds go after they've been,

where light once here is now, what, like the joke,
is bigger than life and blue all over, or brown all over,

here where I am. How big my feet seem, how curiously
solid my body. Turning in bed at night with you gone, alone here,

looking out at the greyish dark, I wonder who else is alive.
Now our bus lumbers on up the hill from the stop at the foot of Queen
‹Street—

another late rain, a thick sky— past the laboring traffic when just across
at an intersection there's another bus going by, its windows

papered with dogs, pictures of dogs, all sizes, kinds and colors,
looking real, patient like passengers, who must be behind

sitting down in the seats. Stupid to ask what things mean if it's only
to doubt them. That was a bus going elsewhere? Ask them.

5

Raining again. Moments ago the sky was a grey lapping pattern
towards the light at the edges still, over Auckland, at the horizon.

It's closed in except for the outline of a darker small cloud
with pleasant, almost lacelike design laid over the lighter sky.

Things to do today. Think of Ted Berrigan, friends absent or dead.
Someone was saying, *you don't really know where you are*

till you move away— "How is it far if you think it." I have still the sense
I've got this body to take care of, a thing someone left me in mind

as it were. Don't forget it. The dogs were there when I went
up to the head of the street to shop for something to eat and a lady,

unaggressively but particular to get there, pushes in to pay for some
‹small items
she's got, saying she wants to get back to her house before the rain.

The sky is pitch-black toward the creek. She's there as I pass with my
‹packages,
she's stopped to peer into some lot has a board enclosure around it,

and there are two dogs playing, bouncing up on each other.
Should I bounce, then, in friendship, against this inquisitive lady,

bark, be playful? One has no real words for that.
Pointless otherwise to say anything she was so absorbed.

6

I can't call across it, see it as a piece, am dulled with its reflective
‹prospect,
want all of it but can't get it, even a little piece here. Hence the dogs,

"The Dogs of Auckland," who were there first walking along with their
‹company,
seemed specific to given streets, led the way, accustomed.

Nothing to do with sheep or herding, no presence other than one
    ‹cannily human,
a scale kept the city particular and usefully in proportion.

When I was a kid I remember lifting my foot up carefully, so as to step
    ‹over
the castle we'd built with blocks. The world here is similar. The sky so
    ‹vast,

so endless the surrounding ocean. No one could swim it.
It's a basic company we've come to.

They say people get to look like their dogs, and if I could,
I'd have been Maggie, thin long nose, yellowish orange hair,

a frenetic mongrel terrier's delight in keeping it going, eager,
vulnerable, but she's gone. All the familiar stories of the old man

and his constant companion, the dog, Bowser.
My pride that Norman Mailer lists *Bob, Son of Battle*

as a book he valued in youth
as I had also. Warm small proud lonely world.

Coming first into this house, from seemingly nowhere
a large brown amiable dog went bounding in

up the steps in front of us, plunged through various rooms
and out. Farther up the street is one less secure, misshapen,

a bit thin-haired where it's worn, twists on his legs, quite small.
This afternoon I thought he'd come out to greet me, coming home.

He was at the curb as I came down and was headed toward me.
Then he got spooked and barked, running, tail down, for his house.

I could hear all the others, back of the doors, howling,
sounding the painful alarm.

7

Empty, vacant. Not the outside but in. What you thought was
a place, you'd determined by talk,

and, turning, neither dogs nor people
were there. Pack up the backdrop. Pull down

the staging. Not "The Dogs" but The Dog of Auckland —
Le Chien d'Auckland, c'est moi!

I am the one with the missing head in the gully
Will saw, walking up the tidal creekbed. I am the one

in the story the friend told, of his Newfoundland,
hit by car at Auckland city intersection, crossing on crosswalk,

knocked down first, then run over, the driver
anxious for repairs to his car. I am the Dog.

Open the sky, let the light back in.
Your ridiculous, pinched faces confound me.

Your meaty privilege, lack of distinguishing measure,
skill, your terrifying, mawkish dependence —

You thought for even one moment it was Your World?
Anubis kills!

8

"Anubis" rhymes with Auckland, says the thoughtful humanist —
at least an "a" begins each word, and from there on it's

only a matter of miles. By now I have certainly noticed
that the dogs aren't necessarily with the people at all, nor are the people

with the dogs. It's the light,
backlit buildings, the huge sense of floating,

platforms of glass like the face
of the one at the edge of Albert Park

reflects (back) the trees, for that charmed
moment all in air. That's where we are.

So how did the dogs get up here, eh?
I didn't even bring myself, much less them.

In the South Island a bull terrier is minding sheep
with characteristic pancake-flat smile.

Meantime thanks, even if now much too late,
to all who move about "down on all fours"

in furry, various coats. Yours was the kind accommodation,
the unobtrusive company, or else the simple valediction of a look.

Edges

Expectably slowed yet unthinking
of outside when in, or weather
as ever more than there when
everything, anything, will be again

Particular, located, familiar in its presence
and reassuring. The end
of the seeming dream was simply
a walk down from the house through the field.

I had entered the edges, static,
had been walking without attention,
thinking of what I had seen, whatever,
a flotsam of recollections, passive reflection.

My own battered body, clamorous
to roll in the grass, sky looming,
the myriad smells ecstatic, felt insistent prick of things
under its weight, wanted something

Beyond the easy, commodious adjustment
to determining thought, the loss of reasons
to ever do otherwise than comply —
tedious, destructive interiors of mind

As whatever came in to be seen,
representative, inexorably chosen,
then left as some judgment.
Here thought had its plan.

Is it only in dreams
can begin the somnambulistic rapture?
Without apparent eyes?
Just simply looking?

All these things were out there
waiting, innumerable, patient.
How could I name even one enough,
call it only a flower or a distance?

If ever, just one moment, a place
I could be in where all imagination would fade
to a center, wondrous, beyond any way
one had come there, any sense,

And the far-off edges of usual
place were inside. Not even the shimmering
reflections, not one even transient ring
come into a thoughtless mind.

Would it be wrong to say, *the sky is up,*
the ground is down, and out there
is what can never be the same—
what, like music, has gone?

Trees stay outside one's thought.
The water stays stable in its shifting.
The road from here to there continues.
One is included.

Here it all is then—
as if expected,
waited for and found
again.

Won't It Be Fine?

At whatever age he was, he was apt with that
"not with a bang but a whimper . . ." Wiseass little
prick felt himself thus projected an impervious
balloon into history. Or maybe not at all so,

just spooked he had blown it again or been blown
out by old-time time's indifference to anything
wouldn't fit the so-called pattern. I am tired, I am
increasingly crippled by my own body's real wear

and tear, and lend my mind to an obsessional search for
les images des jeunes filles or again not so
young at all with huge tits, or come-hither looks,
or whatever my failing head now projects as desirable.

What was I looking at sunk once full weight onto others,
some of whom I hardly knew or even wanted to, mean-
minded bastard that I was and must perforce continue
to be. God help us all who have such fathers, or lovers,

as I feel myself to have been, be, and think to spend
quiet evenings at home while he (me), or they, plural,
pad the feral passages, still in their bedroom slippers,
never dressing anymore but peering out, distracted,

for the mailman, the fellow with the packages, the persons
having the wrong address, or even an unexpected friend appearing.
"No, I never go out anymore, having all I need right here"—
and looks at his wife, children, the dog, as if they were only

a defense. Because where he has been and is cannot admit them.
He has made a tediously contrived "thing to do today" with
his own thing, short of cutting it off. There is no hope in hope,
friends. If you have friends, be sure you are good to them.

Signs

1

The old ones say, "The peach keeps its fuzz until it dies." It seemed for
years as if one would never grow up, never be the first to say anything.
But time is like a river, rather, a dank, sluggish rush, and here one is at
last as anticipated old on its nether bank. I stand there bewildered, in my
pajamas, shouting, "The stone is an apple before it's got hard!" *The ground
is the bottom of the sky.*

2

It begins with I stand there. The old ones say, "The speech keeps its fizz until it dries." For years and years one never grew up, never first or last. But was like a river rather, a dark whoosh, and there was at last one old anticipated on the dark bank. *I* stands there in my pajamas. Shouts, *apple stone hard's got! Hands wrought, God's bought—* Bodies! The sky is ground at the bottom.

3

The. Bod. Ies. Han. Ds. God. S. Bough. T.
(Ic. An. *Read*.) Ston. Es. St. And. Sh. Out. T. Here.
Sky. See. Is. At. T. He. Har. Ds.

It was no friend of mine they shot they caught no friend of mine they sought they thought they fought. Alone on the far bank old now to be there he ought not . . .

Ought not.

Got. Bot. (Of) Tom. The Sky. (Of) God. The Eye.
Bot. Tom. Each. Sp. Eech. P. Each. Lies lie.

4

I cannot tell the truth anymore. I am too old to remember by what right or wrong one was then to be the measure, so as to think that if this, of two, might be down, then that, of one, would be up. The birds make the lovely music just outside the opened windows as we lie there on the freshly made beds in the attractive *chambres des* dispossessed. Or maid or *made*. Make *Mary* dirty man! *This is Hull nor are you out of it,* saith.

5

"He ate the Hull thing." I lied when I told you I was lying. Clean sheets for dirty bodies, God's dotties, odd's potties. Where's the far bank on the corner of. Neither lip's invitation. I can't see the water for the sky. Each year's a peach, hard, and no friend. Bought or sought or fought or caught. What ever happened to rabbits? Did we finally eat them all?

Sieh' D' Rahm!

I need some "water" at this point
where "sky" meets "ground"
—to lead one reader on,
and so a wandering mind anoint . . .

6

Watery disposition. Spongy, rubbery surfaces. Sinking ground. Nowhere one sensible, solid support. Looks up from within the well's depth. Looks out from the edge of the prospect. Down, in. Up, out. Light. Dark. I remember we were sitting on the rock in the clearing. We were standing by the dock near the mooring. Lock of door shutting. Clock's ticking. Walks thinking. Thinner than one was. Aging beginner, sinner. Talks.

7

You have never had chance to speak of how particularly love mattered in your life, nor of the many ways it so invaded you, chafed, rubbed, itched, "grew wet with desire," long, soft, hard, etc. You were observant of cares in such matters, bulks of person, legs, arms, heads, etc. It's hard to budge the real if it's not your own. *Born very young into a world already very old* . . . Even spitting it out was often awkward. Seemingly unseemly, uncertain. Curtain. Hide it from view, then, until they've all gone.

8

What was it friend said? "We are the old ones now!" But that was years ago. Sitting right there where you are. I was. He is. Time's like a rover we'll go no more of. Apple's at bottom of bushel turned to stone. *But I am tired of apples speaking now* . . . Peaches. Faded speeches. Fuzz turned to screaming sirens and old dead men. Dank river darkened in dusk of dead ends. Hits bottom.

Echo's Arrow

FOR JACKSON MAC LOW

Were there answers where they were
  There where air was everywhere
    Time to make impassioned stir
      Place to find an answer for

      Place to find an answer for
    Time to make impassioned stir
  There where air was everywhere
Were there answers where they were

Old Poems

One wishes the *herd* still wound its way
to mark the end of the departing day
or that the road were *a ribbon of moonlight*
tossed between something cloudy (?) or that *the night*

were still something to be walked in like a lake
or that even a bleak stair *down which the blind*
were *driven* might still prove someone's fate—
and pain and love as always still *unkind.*

My shedding body, skin soft as a much worn
leather glove, head empty as an emptied winter pond,
collapsing arms, hands looking like stubble, rubble,
outside still those barns of my various childhood,

the people I still hold to, mother, my grandfather,
grandmother, my sister, the frames of necessary love,
the ones defined me, told me who I was or what I am
and must now learn to let go of, give entirely away.

There cannot be less of me than there was,
not less of things I'd thought to save, or forgot,
placed in something I lost, or ran after,
saw disappear down a road itself is no longer there.

Pump on, old heart. Stay put, vainglorious blood,
red as the something something.
"Evening comes and comes . . ." What
was that great poem about *the man against*

the sky just at the top of the hill
with the last of the vivid sun still behind him
and one couldn't tell
whether he now went up or down?

Mitch

Mitch was a classmate
later married extraordinary poet
and so our families were friends
when we were all young
and lived in New York, New Hampshire, France.

He had eyes with whites
above eyeballs looked out
over lids in droll surmise —
"gone under earth's lid" was Pound's phrase,
cancered stomach?

A whispered information over phone,
two friends the past week . . . ,
the one, she says, an eccentric dear woman,
conflicted with son?
Convicted with ground

tossed in, one supposes,
more dead than alive.
Life's done all it could
for all of them.
Time to be gone?

Not since 1944–45
have I felt so dumbly, utterly,
in the wrong place at
entirely the wrong time,
caught then in that merciless war,

now trapped here, old, on a blossoming earth,
nose filled with burgeoning odors,
wind a caress, sound blurred reassurance,
echo of others, the lovely compacting
human warmths, the eye closing upon you,

seeing eye, sight's companion, dark or light,
makes out of its lonely distortions
it's you again, coming closer, feel
weight in the bed beside me,
close to my bones.

They told me it would be
like this but who could
believe it, not to leave, not to
go away? "I'll hate to
leave this earthly paradise . . ."

There's no time like the present,
no time in the present. Now it floats, goes out like a boat
upon the sea. Can't we see,
can't we now be company
to that one of us

has to go? *Hold my hand, dear.*
I should have hugged him,
taken him up, held him,
in my arms. I should
have let him know I was here.

Is it my turn now,
who's to say or wants to?
You're not sick, there are
certainly those older.
Your time will come.

In God's hands it's cold.
In the universe it's an empty, echoing silence.
Only us to make sounds,
but I made none.
I sat there like a stone.

Three
LIFE & DEATH
THERE
INSIDE MY HEAD

Life & Death

"IF I HAD THOUGHT . . ."
If I had thought
one moment
to reorganize life
as a particular pattern,
to outwit distance, depth,
felt dark was myself
and looked for the hand
held out to me, I
presumed. It grew by itself.

.

It had seemed diligence,
a kind of determined
sincerity, just to keep going,
mattered, people would care
you were there.
I hadn't thought of death—
or anything that happened
simply because it happened.
There was no reason there.

"OH MY GOD . . ."
Oh my god— You
are a funny face
and your smile
thoughtful, your teeth
sharp— The agonies
of simple existence
lifted me up. But
the mirror I looked in
now looks back.

.

It wasn't God
but something else
was at the end,
I thought, would
get you like
my grandpa dead
in coffin
was gone forever,
so they said.

"OUT HERE . . ."
Out here there
is a soundless float
and the earth
seems far below—
or out. The stars
and the planets
glow on the wall.
Inside each one
we fuck, we fuck.

.

But I didn't mean to,
I didn't dare to look.
The first time couldn't
even find the hole
it was supposed to go in—
Lonely down here
in simple skin,
lonely, lonely
without you.

"SEAR AT THE CENTER . . ."
Sear at the center,
convoluted, tough passage,
history's knots,
the solid earth—
What streaked
consciousness, faint
design so secured
semen's spasm,
made *them?*

     ·

I didn't know then,
had only an avarice
to tear open
love and eat its person,
feeling confusion,
driven, wanting
inclusion, hunger
to feel, smell, taste
her flesh.

"IN THE DIAMOND . . ."
In the diamond
above earth,
over the vast, inchoate,
boiling *material*
plunging up, cresting
as a forming cup, on the truncated
legs of a man stretched out,
the hub of penis alert,
once again the story's told.

.

Born very young into a world
already very old, Zukofsky'd said.
I heard the jokes
the men told
down by the river, swimming.
What are you
supposed to do
and how do you learn.
I feel the same way now.

"THE LONG ROAD . . ."
The long road of it all
is an echo,
a sound like an image
expanding, frames growing
one after one in ascending
or descending order, all
of us a rising, falling
thought, an explosion
of emptiness soon forgotten.

.

As a kid I wondered
where do they go,
my father dead. The place
had a faded dustiness
despite the woods and all.
We all grew up.
I see our faces
in old school pictures.
Where are we now?

"WHEN IT COMES . . ."
When it comes,
it loses edge,
has nothing around it,
no place now present
but impulse not one's own,
and so empties into a river
which will flow on
into a white cloud
and be gone.

.

Not me's going!
I'll hang on till
last wisp of mind's
an echo, face shreds
and moldering hands,
and all of whatever
it was can't say
any more to
anyone.

There

Then when those shades so far from us had run
That they could now be seen no more, arose
A new thought in me and then another one,
And many and divers others sprang from those,
And I so wandered in and out of them
That all the wandering made mine eyes to close,
And thinking was transmuted into dream.

–DANTE, *PURGATORIO*

THERE
The wall is at
    What I never said
the beginning faint
    what I couldn't touch

faces between thin
    was me in you
edges of skin
    you in me

an aching determination
    dumb sad pain
inside and out
    wasted blame

thought
    the edge I battered
feeling
    trying to get in

of places things
    away from myself
they are in or are
    locked in doubt

between all this
only myself
and that too again.
trying still to get out.

FEARFUL LOVE
Love was my heart
No one cares
in the pit
even feels

in the dark
the stares
was my fear
the evil

in the coil
I screamed to myself
of the near
turned into picture

of another where
saw only myself
a congress of birds
in the sullen mirror

waited to hear
had become one of them
what a gun could say
fixed in a form

to a simple world what the white
abstract dead
faced one now would say.
out of my head.

LOOP
I left it behind
    Only me
in the dark
    like they say

for others to find
    no one more
as they came in
    than another

two and two
    if there
the doubles of desire
    it's enough

their bodies' architecture
    inside flesh
myself still inside
    I could be

singing small grey bird
    more than reflection
caught by design
    fixed as an echo

upright cock breast
    be myself more
hips the rope's loop.
    like passage like door.

HAND
This way to end
> *Comes too close*
an outstretched hand
> *to me frightens*

reaches forward to find
> *stuns what I feel*
place for itself
> *argues existence*

fingers grown large
> *makes me confused*
in eye's disposition
> *makes pattern of place*

opaque dark
> *textures of patience*
skirt's billowing pattern
> *all afterthought*

there on the palm
> *destructive bored*
perched on finger
> *else pulses behind*

bird looks out
> *comes forward to find*
secure in its doubt.
> *grabs on to my mind.*

BODY
What twisting thought
I'd been taken
holds in place
held driven

parts of mind
brought fixed
body's found
displaced in reflection

makes grace weight
love sounded
hangs head down
included secured

stands behind puts out
made me other
arms with their hands
than simplifying thought

whether up or down
broken out doubling cock
here come to rest
head hung faceless

one and another
down hands
at last together.
held me held me.

Inside My Head

INSIDE MY HEAD
Inside my head a common room,
a common place, a common tune,
a common wealth, a common doom

inside my head. I close my eyes.
The horses run. Vast are the skies,
and blue my passing thoughts' surprise

inside my head. What is this space
here found to be, what is this place
if only me? Inside my head, whose face?

THE TOOLS
First there, it proves to be still here.
Distant as seen, it comes then to be near.
I found it here and there unclear.

What if my hand had only been
extension of an outside reaching in
to work with common means to change me then?

All things are matter, yet these seem
caught in the impatience of a dream,
locked in the awkwardness they mean.

THE SWAN
Peculiar that *swan* should mean *a sound?*
I'd thought of gods and power, and wounds.
But here in the curious quiet this one has settled down.

All day the barking dogs were kept at bay.
Better than dogs, a single swan, they say,
will keep all such malignant force away

and so preserve a calm, make pond a swelling lake—
sound through the silent grove a shattering spate
of resonances, jarring the mind awake.

THE ROSE
Into one's self come in again,
here as if ever now to once again begin
with beauty's old, old problem never-ending—

Go, lovely rose . . . So was the story told
in some extraordinary place then, *once upon a time* so old
it seems an echo now as it again unfolds.

I point to *me* to look out at the world.
I see the white, white petals of this rose unfold.
I know such beauty in the world grows cold.

THE SKULL
"Come closer. Now there is nothing left
either inside or out to gainsay death,"
the skull that keeps its secrets saith.

The ways one went, the forms that were
empty as wind and yet they stirred
the heart to its passion, all is passed over.

Lighten the load. Close the eyes.
Let the mind loosen, the body die,
the bird fly off to the opening sky.

THE STAR
Such space it comes again to be,
a room of such vast possibility,
a depth so great, a way so free.

Life and its person, thinking to find
a company wherewith to keep the time
a peaceful passage, a constant rhyme,

stumble perforce, must lose their way,
know that they go too far to stay
stars in the sky, children at play.

If I were writing this

One

The Way

Somewhere in all the time that's passed
was a thing in mind became the evidence,
the pleasure even in fact of being lost
so quickly, simply that what it was could never last.

Only knowing was measure of what one could
make hold together for that moment's recognition,
or else the world washed over like a flood
of meager useless truths, of hostile incoherence.

Too late to know that knowing was its own reward
and that wisdom had at best a transient credit.
Whatever one did or didn't do was what one could.
Better at last believe than think to question?

There wasn't choice if one had seen the light,
not of belief but of that soft, blue-glowing fusion
seemed to appear or disappear with thought,
a minute magnesium flash, a firefly's illusion.

Best wonder at mind and let that flickering ambience
of wondering be the determining way you follow,
which leads itself from day to day into tomorrow,
finds all it ever finds is there by chance.

The American Dream

Edges and disjuncts, shattered, bitter planes,
a wedge of disconsolate memories to anchor fame,
fears of the past, a future still to blame—

Multiple heavens, hells, nothing is straight.
You earn your money, then you wait
for so-called life to see that you get paid.

Tilt! Again it's all gone wrong.
This is a heartless, hopeless song.
This is an empty, useless song.

Names

Marilyn's was Norma Jean.
Things are not always what they seem.
Skin she lived back of like some screen

kept her wonder in common view,
said what she did, you could too,
loved by many, touched by few.

She married heroes of all kinds
but no one seemed to know her mind,
none the secret key could find.

Scared kid, Norma Jean?
Are things really what they seem?
What is it that beauty means?

Twenty-five

Balling the Jack   Down the Track
Won't Be Back   Too Late, Jack

See the rush of light—
Time's flight, out of sight.

Feel the years like tears—
the days gone away.

(Lemons) Pear Appears

If it's there, it's something—
And when you see it,
Not just your eyes know it.
It's yourself, like they say, you bring.

These words, these seemingly rounded
Forms—looks *like* a pear? *Is* yellow?
Where's *that* to be found—
In some abounding meadow?

Like likes itself, sees similarities
Everywhere it goes.
But what that means,
Nobody knows.

Dried Roses

"Dried roses . . ." Were these from some walk
All those years ago? Were you the one
Was with me? Did we talk?
Who else had come along?

Memory can stand upright
Like an ordered row of stiff stems,
Dead echo of flowering heads,
Roses once white, pink and red.

Back of them the blackness,
Backdrop for all our lives,
The wonders we thought to remember
Still life, still life.

Drawn & Quartered

1
Speed is what's needed.
Move quick before depleted
of more than a battered leg will prove.
Go for it—as in love.

2
Hold still, lion!
I am trying
to paint you
while there's time to.

3
We have common sense
and common bond.
That's enough
to get along.

4
Have you known each other long?
Long before you were born!
Have you both been happy in marriage?
I think it's proven a commodious carriage.

5
Are they together?
Grandmother and granddaughter?
Is there some fact of pain
in their waiting?

6
Am I only material
for you to feel?
Is that all you see
when you look at me?

7
Image of self at earlier age —
when thoughts had gone inward,
and life became an emptying page —
myself moving toward nothing.

8
Why not tell
what you've kept a secret
not wait for it
to leap out?

9
Dear cat, I see you
and will attend
and feed you
now as then.

10
Here I sit
meal on lap
come to eat
just like that!

11
There's someone
behind
black eye covers,
smothered.

12
Closes, as an echo—
The shoulder, mouth, rounded
head—Two more, to say
each wanted it that way?

13
We sat like this
the night we went away—
just us two, in this same place,
and the boat on the ocean blue.

14
For years I'd thought
such bliss as this could not be bought.
While I waited,
my desire itself abated.

15
Something hot to drink.
God knows what's in it.
Waking or sleeping
in no one's keeping.

16
You displaced me by your singing.
My ears were ringing!
My fingers were glue
as each note rang true.

17
"Man, this stuff
is rough!"
"What would you pay
to make it go way?"

18
Still asleep or else dead.
Take him to bed.
He'll wake up in the morning
and I'll be gone.

19
Angel holding up
the roof top —
else would fall
and kill us all!

20
One word
    I heard
you said
    you read.

21
Mabel had come
all the way to town
to stand as you see her
and jump up and down.

22
Mine it was
and mine it will be—

No *because*
and never a *maybe*!

*Mine it was
and mine it will be* . . .

23
My only horse is dead,
who was my whole farmstead,
its entire provenance and agent.
Life has no further occasion.

24
Beyond, I hope, desire—
free of the entangling fire—
I lay me down to sleep.
Read it and weep!

25
"Too deep for words"—
My weary hand was poised
Above the paper's blank—
too white for thoughts, recalcitrant for tears.

26
What a complicated argument,
whether wrong or right!
Where's the fun
in being simply one?

27
He says the enemy's won—
and we can go home!
The drum beats
in the empty street.

28
Somewhere here it said
that *life is like a river*—
but look as hard as I can, I never
find it again—or anything else instead.

29
And have you read
my verses clear
and may I now
call you *my dear?*

30
All these pages
to turn,
all the bridges
to burn.

31
What I do
Is my own business.
No use looking.
You'll see nothing.

32
If music be
enough for you
lend me ears
so I can hear too.

33
Let me try that too
and see if I sound like you—
or is it your body's song
pulls things along?

34
When you are done
we can play!
Outside the day waits
until the sun goes down.

35
Oh little one,
what are you eating?
Bottle emptied beside you,
nought left but your thumb?

36
It was still in front of them
but soon began to be gone.
Look, said one, now it's going!
Still, they thought, it will come again.

37
Statue? Hermione's—
A Winter's Tale—
in the garden fixed
sense of beauty's evident patience.

38
Maybe this uniform's better,
Maybe this time I'll be the winner.
Maybe I'll shoot straighter.
Maybe they'll get dead first.

39
From the wars I've come,
following the drum,
cannon's bombast,
the military brass asses.

40
Love's the other
in the tunnel—
looks back
down the track.

41
Mother of her country,
keeping the dullards at bay,
forcing the boys to pay,
taking the fences away.

42
It's two o'clock
but we can't stop!
We couldn't then
when we drank the gin.

43
If I had a cent you'd have it.
But I don't.
If I knew what to do,
I'd tell you.

44
Your thought of me is so dear.
All I feel clears
in your own warm heart
and your eyes opened wide.

45
No animal would undertake
such a foolish isolation,
need to forgo a common dinner
so as not to be a common sinner.

46
Your cut, friend.
Is it, then?
Will you cheat again?
Let's see who wins.

47
On such a night,
as I may have told you,
the moon shone bright
and I grew older.

48
What will you shoot with that?
A rabbit!
Well, where will you find it?
Behind you!

49
The tea's cold,
cups still on other table.
The house is quiet
with no one inside it.

50
Like a circle,
uncoiling like a spring,
up and down and then around,
stairs are resourceful.

51
Summer's over?
Where was I
when it first came
bringing such pleasure?

52
"Miles to go"
but no snow
at least nor is it too long
till I'm safe at home.

53
Here browse the cows.
The gentle herdsman stands apart.
So nature's provenance
attends its art.

54
Finally to have come
to where one had so long wanted to visit
and then to stand
there and look at it.

Life

FOR GAEL

Where have we drifted,
Or walked and talked our way into,
When it was attention we both thought to offer
All that we came to?

I can see you with your wee brush poised
To make the first crucial dab
Will encompass the wondering desert,
Marveling to find such witness.

Seriousness is its own reward?
It wasn't ever innocence,
·   Or a diffidence or indifference.
Not timidity ever.

Comment allez-vous, mate?
Like the last Canadian
Learned French at last to
Make friends too late?

But you had left long ago
And as all here I missed you,
Still acknowledging friend of my life,
Still true.

Millay's Echoes

"All I could see from where I stood
Was three long mountains and a wood;
I turned and looked the other way,
And saw three islands in a bay.
So with my eyes I traced the line

Of the horizon, thin and fine,
Straight around till I was come
Back to where I'd started from;
And all I saw from where I stood
Was three long mountains and a wood . . ."

Was three long mountains and a wood . . .
The emptying disposition stood,
The empty, echoing mind struck dumb,
The body's loss of kingdoms come,
Of suns, too many, long gone down,
And on that place precise she'd stood
Little was left to tell of time
Except the proof she *traced a line*
To make a poem *so with my eyes* . . .
of the horizon, thin and fine . . .

The circle held and here again
One sees what then she'd pointed to —
"Three islands in a bay," she said,
Much like that emptiness she knew,
The vaguest light, the softest mist
Hid them from sight. So fades at last
Whatever water will know best.
All proof seems pointless in such world,
Seems painful now to bring to mind.

Yet how forget that she once stood
Where now I do in altering time
And saw three mountains and a wood,
And pounding surf far down below
Where, when I look to see in kind
"The three long mountains and a wood,"
They are still there and still the sea
Beats back to me this monody.

For Hannah's Fourteenth Birthday

What's heart to say
as days pass,
what's a mind to know
after all?

What's it mean to be wise
or right,
if time's still
insistent master?

But if you doubt the track,
still don't look back.
Let the love you bring
find its fellow.

Girl to young woman,
world's well begun.
All comes true
just for you.

Trust heart's faith
wherever it goes.
It still knows
you follow.

For Will

I was at the door,
still standing as if waiting for more—
but not knowing what for.

Was I with you?
Already we'd come a long distance together.
It was time now for something other.

In my head a story echoed
someone had told me
of how a son and father

came to a like doorway.
Then, in seeming anger, the son dragged the father out,
through an orchard, until the father shouted,

"Only this far *I* dragged *my* father! No more!
Put me down . . ." Was this to be their parting,
the last word? Was it only to be *gone*

each could think of, then, as each other?
All their time together, silent, warm,
knowing without thinking one another's mind,

no end to such—
could there be?
No, there was no end to it.

Always life was the constant
and one held it, gave it
one to another,

saw it go in that instant,
with love,
with all that one knows.

No riddle to that
except there is no end until it comes,
no friends but those one's found.

"Wild Nights, Wild Nights"

It seemed your friend
Had finally others to attend.
My time was yours alone to spend.

I leaned against the fence and waited.
Our love, I felt, was unequivocally fated.
To go sans word would leave all still unstated.

Hence scurrying hopes and pledge at last! Now here—
With all the fading years
Between—I wonder where

Time ever was before we
Walked in those towering woods, beneath the ample clouds,
Bathed in that wondrous air!

"When I Heard the Learn'd Astronomer . . ."

FOR ALLEN

A bitter twitter,
flitter,
of birds
in evening's
settling,
a reckoning
beckoning,
someone's getting
some sad news,
the birds gone to nest,
to roost
in the darkness,

asking no improvident questions,
none singing,
no *hark*,
no *lark*,
nothing in the quiet dark.

Begun with like hypothesis,
arms, head, shoulders,
with body state
better soon than late,
better not wait,
better not be late,
breathe ease,
fall to knees
in posture of compliance,
obeisance,
accommodation
a motivation.
All systems must be imagination
which works,
albeit have quirks.

Add by the one
or by the none,
make it by *either*
or *or.*
Or say that after you
I go.
Or say you
follow me.
See what comes after
or before,
what
you had thought.

Many's a twenty?
A three?
Is twenty-three
plenty?

A call to reason
then
in due season,
a proposal of heaven
at seven
in the evening,
a cup of tea, a sense
of recompense
for anyone works for a living,
getting and giving.

Does it seem mind's all?
What's it mean
to be inside
a circle, to fly
in the sky, dear bird?

Words scattered,
tattered,
yet
said
make it
all evident,
manifest.
No contest.
One's one again.
It's done.

Hurry on, friend.
There is no end
to desire,
to Blake's fire,
to Beckett's mire,
to any such whatever.

Old friend's dead
in bed.

Old friends die.
Goodbye!

"Where Late the Sweet Birds Sang . . ."

FOR DON

Blunted efforts as the distance
Becomes insistent,
A divided time between now and then,
Between oneself and old friend—

Because what I'd thought age was,
Was a lessening, a fading
Reach to something not clearly seen,
But there still in memory.

No one thought it could be fun.
But— *Well begun is half done?*
Half gone, then it's all gone,
All of it over.

Now no one seems there anymore.
Each day, which had been a pleasure,
Becomes a fear someone else is dead,
Someone knocking at the door.

Born very young into a world already very old . . .
Always the same story
And I was told.
So now it's for me.

Two

En Famille

FOR ELLIE

I wandered lonely as a cloud . . .
I'd seemingly lost the crowd
I'd come with, family—father, mother, sister and brothers—
fact of a common blood.

Now there was no one,
just my face in the mirror, coat on a single hook,
a bed I could make getting out of.
Where had they gone?

.

What was that vague determination
cut off the nurturing relation
with all the density, this given company—
what made one feel such desperation

to get away, get far from home, be gone from those
would know us even if they only saw our noses or our toes,
accept with joy our helpless mess,
taking for granted it was part of us?

.

My friends, hands on each other's shoulders,
holding on, keeping the pledge
to be for one, for all, a securing center,
no matter up or down, or right or left—

to keep the faith, keep happy, keep together,
keep at it, so keep on
despite the fact of necessary drift.
Home might be still the happiest place on earth?

.

You won't get far by yourself.
It's dark out there.
There's a long way to go.
The dog knows.

It's him loves us most,
or seems to, in dark nights of the soul.
Keep a tight hold.
Steady, we're not lost.

.

Despite the sad vagaries,
anchored in love, placed in the circle,
young and old, a round—
love's fact of this bond.

One day one will look back
and think of them—
where they were, now gone—
remember it all.

.

Turning inside as if in dream,
the twisting face I want to be my own,
the people loved and with me still,
I see their painful faith.

Grow, dears, then fly away!
But when the dark comes, then come home.
Light's in the window, heart stays true.
Call—and I'll come to you.

.

The wind blows through the shifting trees
outside the window, over the fields below.
Emblems of growth, of older, younger,
of towering size or all the vulnerable hope

as echoes in the image of these three
look out with such reflective pleasure,
so various and close. They stand there,
waiting to hear a music they will know.

.

I like the way you both look out at me.
Somehow it's sometimes hard to be a human.
Arms and legs get often in the way,
making oneself a bulky, awkward burden.

Tell me your happiness is simply true.
Tell me I can still learn to be like you.
Tell me the truth is what we do.
Tell me that care for one another is the clue.

.

We're here because there's nowhere else to go,
we've come in faith we learned as with all else.
Someone once told us and so it is we know.
No one is left outside such simple place.

No one's too late, no one can be too soon.
We comfort one another, making room.
We dream of heaven as a climbing stair.
We look at stars and wonder why and where.

.

Have we told you all you'd thought to know?
Is it really so quickly now the time to go?
Has anything happened you will not forget?
Is where you are enough for all to share?

Is wisdom just an empty word?
Is age a time one might finally well have missed?
Must humanness be its own reward?
Is happiness this?

For You

At the edge, fledgling,
hypocrite reader, *mon frère,*
mon semblable, there
you are me?

Conversion to Her

Parts of each person,
Lumber of bodies,
Heads and legs
Inside the echoes—

I got here slowly
Coming out of my mother,
Herself in passage
Still wet with echoes—

Little things surrounding,
Little feet, little eyes,
Black particulars,
White disparities—

Who was I then?
What man had entered?
Was my own person
Passing pleasure?

My body shrank,
Breath was constricted,
Head confounded,
Tongue muted.

I wouldn't know you,
Self in old mirror.
I won't please you
Crossing over.

Knife cuts through.
Things stick in holes.
Spit covers body.
Head's left hanging.

Hole is in middle.
Little boy wants one.
Help him sing here
Helpless and wanting.

.

My odor?
My name?
My flesh?
My shame?

My other
than you are,
my way out—
My door shut—

In silence this
happens, in pain.

.

Outside is empty.

Inside is a house
of various size.

Covered with skin
one lives within.

Women are told
to let world unfold.

Men, to take it,
make or break it.

All's true
except for you.

.

Being human, one wonders at the others,
men with their beards and anger,

women with their friends and pleasure—
and the children they engender together—

until the sky goes suddenly black and a monstrous thing
comes from nowhere upon them

in their secure slumbers, in their righteous undertakings,
shattering thought.

One cannot say, *Be as women,*
be peaceful, then. The hole from which we came

isn't metaphysical.
The one to which we go is real.

Surrounding a vast space
seems boundless appetite

in which a man still lives
till he become a woman.

Clemente's Images

1
Sleeping birds, lead me,
soft birds, be me

inside this black room,
back of the white moon.

In the dark night
sight frightens me.

2

Who is it nuzzles there
with furred, round-headed stare?

Who, perched on the skin,
body's float, is holding on?

What other one stares still,
plays still, on and on?

3

Stand upright, prehensile,
squat, determined,

small guardians of the painful
outside coming in —

in stuck-in vials with needles,
bleeding life in, particular, heedless.

4

Matrix of world
upon a turtle's broad back,

carried on like that,
eggs as pearls,

flesh and blood and bone
all borne along.

5

I'll tell you what you want,
to say a word,

to know the letters in yourself,
a skin falls off,

a big eared head appears,
an eye and mouth.

6
Under watery here,
under breath, under duress,

understand a pain
has threaded a needle with a little man—

gone fishing.
And fish appear.

7
If small were big,
if then were now,

if here were there,
if find were found,

if mind were all there was,
would the animals still save us?

8
A head was put
upon the shelf got took

by animal's hand and stuck
upon a vacant corpse

who, blurred, could nonetheless
not ever be the quietly standing bird it watched.

9
Not lost,
not better or worse,

much must of necessity depend on resources,
the pipes and bags brought with us

inside, all the sacks
and how and to what they are or were attached.

10
Everybody's child
walks the same winding road,

laughs and cries, dies.
That's "everybody's child,"

the one who's in between
the others who have come and gone.

11
Turn as one will, the sky will always be
far up above the place he thinks to dream as earth.

There float the heavenly
archaic persons of primordial birth,

held in the scan of ancient serpent's tooth,
locked in the mind as when it first began.

12
Inside I am the other of a self,
who feels a presence always close at hand,

one side or the other, knows another one
unlocks the door and quickly enters in.

Either as or, we live a common person.
Two is still one. It cannot live apart.

13
Oh, weep for me—
all from whom life has stolen

hopes of a happiness stored
in gold's ubiquitous pattern,

in tinkle of commodious, enduring money,
else the bee's industry in hives of golden honey.

14
He is safely put
in a container, head to foot,

and there, on his upper part, wears still
remnants of a life he lived at will—

but, lower down, he probes at that doubled sack
holds all his random virtues in a mindless fact.

15
The forms wait, swan,
elephant, crab, rabbit, horse, monkey, cow,

squirrel and crocodile. From the one
sits in empty consciousness, all seemingly has come

and now it goes, to regather,
to tell another story to its patient mother.

16
Reflection reforms, each man's a life,
makes its stumbling way from mother to wife—

cast as a gesture from ignorant flesh,
here writes in fumbling words to touch,

say, *how can I be,*
when she is all that was ever me?

17
Around and in—
And up and down again,

and far and near—
and here and there,

in the middle is
a great round nothingness.

18
Not metaphoric,
flesh is literal earth

turns to dust
as all the body must,

becomes the ground
wherein the seed's passed on.

19
Entries, each foot feels its own way,
echoes passage in persons,

holds the body upright,
the secret of thresholds, lintels,

opening body above it,
looks up, looks down, moves forward.

20
Necessity, the mother of invention,
father of intention,

sister to brother to sister, to innumerable others,
all one as the time comes,

death's appointment,
in the echoing head, in the breaking heart.

21
In self one's place defined,
in heart the other find.

In mind discover *I*,
in body find the sky.

Sleep in the dream as one,
wake to the others there found.

22
Emptying out
each complicating part,

each little twist of mind inside,
each clenched fist,

each locked, particularizing thought,
forgotten, emptying out.

23
What did it feel like
to be one at a time—

to be caught in a mind
in the body you'd found

in yourself alone—
in each other one?

24
Broken hearts, a curious round of echoes—
and there behind them the old garden

with its faded, familiar flowers,
where all was seemingly laced together—

a trueness of true,
a blueness of blue.

25
The truth is in a container
of no size or situation.

It has nothing
inside

Worship—
Warship. Sail away.

As If

As if a feeling, come from nought,
Suspended time in fascinated concentration,
So that all the world therein became
Of that necessity its own reward—

I lifted to mind a piece
Of bright blue air and then another.
Then clouds in fluffy substance floated by.
Below I felt a lake of azure waited.

I cried, *Here,* here *I am—the only place I'll ever be* . . .
Whether it made a common sense or found a world,
Years flood their gate, the company dispersed.
This person still is me.

Possibilities

FOR SUSAN ROTHENBERG

What do you wear?
How does it feel
to wear clothes?
What shows
what you were or where?

This accident, accidental, person,
feeling out, feelings out—
outside the box one's in—
skin's resonances, reticent romances,
the blotch of recognition, blush?

It's a place one's going,
going out to, could reach
out just so far to be at the edge
of it all, there, no longer inside,
waiting, expectant, a confused thing.

One wanted skin to walk in,
be in. One wanted each leg to stand,
both hands to have substance,
both eyes to look out, recognize,
all of it, closer and closer.

Put it somewhere, one says.
Put it down. But it's not a thing
simply. It's all of it here,
all of it near and dear,
everywhere one is, this and that.

Inside, it could have been included.
There was room for the world.
One could think of it, even be simple, ample.
But not "multitudes," not that way *in* —
It's out, *out*, one's going. Loosed.

Still — wistful in heaven, happy in hell?
Sky was an adamant wall,
earth a compact of dirty places,
faces of people one used to know.
Air — smell, sound and taste — was still wonderful.

One dreamed of a thoughtless moment,
the street rushing forward, heads up.
One willed almost a wave of silence
to hear the voices underneath.
Each layer, each particular, recalled.

But now to be *here?*
Putting my hand on the table,
I watch it turn into wood,
Fibrous, veins like wood's grain,
But not that way separated—all one.

I felt a peace come back.
No longer needed to say what it was,
nothing left somehow to name only—
still was each each, all all,
evident mass, bulky sum, a complex accumulation?

My mother dying sat up, ecstatic,
coming out of the anesthetic, said,
"It's all free! *You don't have to pay
for any of it . . .*" It's there
if you can still get to it?

Come closer, *closer.* Come as near
as you can get. Let me know
each edge, each shelf of act,
all the myriad colors, all the shimmering presences,
each breath, finger of odor, echoed pin drop.

Adumbrate nature. Walk a given path.
You are as much its fact as any other.
You stand a scale far smaller than a tree's.
A mountain makes you literal as a pebble.
Look hard for what it is you want to see.

The sky seems in its heavens, laced with cloud.
The horizon's miles and miles within one's sight.
Cooling, earth gathers in for night.
Birds quiet, stars start out in the dark.
Wind drops. Thus life itself can settle.

Nothing's apart from all and seeing is
the obvious beginning of an act
can only bring one closer to the art
of *being* closer. So feeling all there is,
one's hands and heart grow full.

For Anya

An "outside" was always what I wanted
to get to, the proverbial opening
in the clearing, plain church with massed,
seated persons, the bright water
dense with white caps and happy children.

Was I late, stupid, to arrive always
as *It's me!*—somehow still alone,
however I'd thought myself present,
muted the persistent self-concerns,
took requisite chances, trying to let go?

Evening's clouds seem a dynasty,
an end forever to such confusion.
Birds sing still at the edges of hearing.
Night settles itself comfortably
far—and once and for all—beyond me.

I think and therefore I am self-conscious.
There are no mirrors here to look into,
No answering reassurances one's sufficient.
The "outside" is empty but vast, I think.
It's everywhere around me and still there.

There (1)

I left the wagon far too soon—
too particular, too big
or small for my britches.

I got off too early,
was too impatient to get there
and didn't even know where I was going.

I wouldn't let the company
count me in, take me with them,
even to a clearly pleasant place.

One by one was for me a confusion.
It was *one* period
I wanted—just *me*, just you—no more.

How does one get back on, brother?
Wherever you're going is fine with me.
Anything I've got is yours and always was.

There (2)

FOR DOUG MESSERLI

Well if ever,
Then when never—

House's round,
Sound's sound.

Here's where
Comes *there*

If you do,
They will too.

Three

Thinking

FOR ALEX

Thought feels the edges.
Just so far it was only yesterday?
So far it seems now till tomorrow.

Time isn't space.
Away for the day, one says—
gone fishing. Now and again.

The sounds echo in the quiet morning—
such faint edges of place, things, not yet quite seen.
But one knows the familiar presences.

The world will be as one left it,
still there, to reappear again perhaps
where it always is.

Cambridge, Mass 1944

Sister remembers
night she'd come down
to meet me in town
my friends then told her

I'd jumped in the river
and hadn't returned.
—But once in the water
I'd kept on swimming

across to far shore
where police fished me out
and put me in jail
where I stayed the night

naked in cell
so clothes could dry out.
Next morning the judge
gave me dime to get home.

Place to Be

Days the weather sits
in the endless sky,
the clouds drifting by.

The winter's snow,
summer's heat,
same street.

Nothing changes
but the faces, the people,
all the things they do

'spite of heaven and hell
or city hall —
Nothing's wiser than a moment.

No one's chance
is simply changed by wishing,
right or wrong.

What you do is how you get along.
What you did is all it ever means.

Pictures

FOR PEN

1

This distance
between pane of glass,
eye's sight—
the far waving green edge

of trees, sun's
reflection, light
yellow—and sky there too
light blue.

2

I will sit here
till breeze, ambient,
enfolds me and I
lift away. I will

sit here as sun
warms my hands, my
body eases, and sounds
grow soft and intimate

in my ears. I will sit
here and the back of the house
behind me will at last
disappear. I will sit here.

3

Harry's gone out for pizza.
Mabel's home all alone.
Mother just left for Ibiza.
Give the old man a bone?

Remember when Barkis was willing?
When onions grew on the lawn?
When airplanes cost just a shilling?
Where have the good times gone?

4
If one look back
or thinks to look
in that uselessly opaque direction,
little enough's ever there.

What is it one stares into,
thinks still to recover
as it all fades out –
mind's vagary?

I call to you brutally.
I remember the day we met
I remember how you sat, impatient
to get out.

Back is no direction . . .
Tout passe?
Life is the river
we've carried with us.

5
Sun's shadows aslant
across opening expansive
various green fields down

from door
here ajar on box tower's
third floor –

look out on
wonder.
This morning.

6

I never met you afterward
nor seemingly knew you before.
Our lives were interfolded,
wrapped like a present.

The odors, the tastes, the surfaces
of our bodies were the map —
the mind a distraction,
trying to keep up.

I could not compare you to anything.
You were not like rhubarb
or clean sheets — or, dear as it might be,
sudden rain in the street.

All those years ago, on the beach in Dover,
with that time so ominous,
and the couple so human,
pledging their faith to one another,

now again such a time seems here —
not to fear
death or what's been so given —
to yield one's own despair.

7

Like sitting in back seat,
can't see what street
we're on or what the
one driving sees

or where we're going.
Waiting for what's to happen,
can't quite hear the conversation,
the big people, sitting up front.

8
Death, be not proud . . .
Days be not done.
Air be not gone.
Head be not cowed.

Bird be not dead.
Thoughts be not fled.
Come back instead,
Heart's hopeful wedding.

Face faint in mirror.
Why does it stay there?
What's become
Of person who was here?

9
Wet
      water
warm
      fire.

Rough
      wood
cold
      stone.

Hot
      coals
shining
      star.

Physical hill still my will.
Mind's ambience alters all.

10

As I rode out one morning
just at break of day
a pain came upon me
unexpectedly —

As I thought one day
not to think anymore,
I thought again,
caught, and could not stop —

Were I the horse I rode,
were I the bridge I crossed,
were I a tree
unable to move,

the lake would have
no reflections,
the sweet, soft air
no sounds.

So I hear, I see,
tell still the echoing story
of all that lives in a forest,
all that surrounds me.

Supper

Shovel it in.
Then go away again.
Then come back and
shovel it in.

Days on the way,
lawn's like a shorn head
and all the chairs are put away
again. Shovel it in.

Eat for strength, for health.
Eat for the hell of it, for
yourself, for country and your mother.
Eat what your little brother didn't.

Be content with your lot
and all you got.
Be whatever they want.
Shovel it in.

I can no longer think of heaven
as any place I want to go,
not even dying. I want
to shovel it in.

I want to keep on eating,
drinking, thinking.
I am ahead. I am not dead.
Shovel it in.

"Short and Clear"

FOR GREGORY, WHO SAID IT

Short and clear, dear—
short and clear.

No need for fear.
All's here.

Keep it
short and clear.

You are the messenger,
the message, the way.

Short and clear, dear,
all the way.

Scholar's Rocks

FOR JIM DINE

1
What has been long pondered,
become encrusted,
grown into itself—

colored by world, by echoed
independence from world,
by all that it wasn't—

what had been thought,
what had been felt,
what was it?

2
As in a forest
as if *as if*
one had come to

as in a forest
to a wall of the heart

a wall
of the heart

3
glass
enclosing including

stuck into
these insistent

Things

4
Ghosts of
another *wall—*

childhood's—
all hung

in order
elegant and particular

hands handed
hand tools

5

What happens when
the house is at last
quiet and the lights
lowered, go finally out?

Then is it all silent?
Are the echoes still,
the reflections faded,
the places left alone?

6

As fingers round a stick,
as a pen's held,
a thumb can help grip,
so a wrench's extension,

a hammer's force,
meticulous cutting clippers,
hatchet's sharpened edge
one could not cut without.

7

I love the long wrench,
whose gears permit a tension
'twixt objects fixed
tight between its iron teeth.

So locked, one can twist
and so the object turns,
loosens, at last comes out.
This is life's bliss!

8
Which
one
did
it?

Do you recognize
the culprit,
is your own heart
full?

9
Sometimes it's like looking at orphans —
and no one will come.

No one seems to want them.
There's a patience, which seems awful —

inhuman to be left,
to have no place on earth?

The heart alone holds them.
Minds made them.

10
Seeing's believing. Beyond eyes, beyond the edges of things. The face of
what's out there is an adamant skin. One touches it, feels it. Coming,
going, *through the looking glass* . . . Leaving marks, making a trail for the
way back. One writes on the surface, sensing all that's under it. Oceans
of a common history. Things of the past.

Bub and Sis

FOR CAROLYN KIZER

Let the dog lie down with the dog,
people with people.
It makes a difference where you fit
and how you feel.

When young, I was everybody's human,
a usual freaked person,
looking for love in the dark,
being afraid to turn the lights on.

It makes a great difference
to have a friend
who's a woman,
when you're a so-called man,

who can talk to you
across the great divide
of mixed signals
and wounded pride.

Small thanks in the end
for that maintaining sister,
but what she says
is what you remember.

For Georg

Art says,
what are you looking at?

But the words want
to say what they have to.

*If there is here
then there's* here *too?*

The grey green monster with
the ugly face isn't here,

the words want to say. But, *look,*
says the image, *right behind you!*

Anthropomorphic instance in any case
is a drag. You don't get reality as choices.

The battle goes on,
pens into ploughshares, canvas into awnings —

or simply faces
in the crowd. I want

a lot of things, the
separables, the x's and y's

of existence. *Upside down,*
says Georg, *is a whole new ballgame!*

The runner
advances to second.

For Gregory Corso

I'll miss you,
who did better than I did
at keeping the faith of poets,
staying true.

It's as if you couldn't
do otherwise,
had always an appetite
waiting to lead.

You kept to the high road
of canny vision,
let the rest of us
find our own provision.

Ruthless, friends felt,
you might take everything.
Nothing was safe from you.
You did what you wanted.

Yet, safe in your words, your poems,
their humor could hold me.
The wit, the articulate
gathering rhythms,

all made a common sense
of the archaic wonders.
You pulled from nowhere the kingly chair.
You sat alone there.

The Heart

FOR PEN

In the construction
of the chest, there is
a heart.

A boat
upon its blood
floats past

and round or down
the stream of life,
the plummeting veins

permit its passage
to admit no gains,
no looking back.

One steps aboard,
one's off.
The ticket taker

signs the time allotted.
Seated, amorphous persons
see no scenery

but feel
a chill about their knees
and hear a fading cry

as all the many sides of life
whiz by,
a blast at best, a loss

of individual impressions.
Still I sit
with you inside me too—

and *us,*
the couple thus encoupled,
ride on into the sweetening dark.

Memory

FOR KEITH AND ROSMARIE

Remember when
we all were ten
and had again
what's always been—

Or if we were,
no fear was there
to cause some stir
or be elsewhere—

Because it's when
all thoughts occur
to say again
we're where we were.

"If I were writing this . . ."

If I were writing this
with prospect of encouragement
or had I begun some work
intended to be what it was

or even then and there it was what
had been started, even now
I no longer thought to wait,
had begun, had found

myself in the time and place
writing words which I knew,
could say *ring, dog, hat, car,*
was rushing, it felt, to keep up

with the trembling impulse,
the connivance the words contrived
even themselves to be though
I wrote them, thought they were me.

     ·

Once in, once out
Turn's a roundabout
Seeing eyes get the nod

Or dog's a mistaken god?
God's a mistaken dog?

Gets you home on time
Rhymes with time on time

In time for two a "t"
begins and ends it.

     ·

A blue grey edge.
Trees line it.
Green field finds it.
Eyes look.

                .

Let the aching heart take over.
Cry till eyes blur.
Be as big as you were.
Stir the pot.

                .

Whenever it's sense,
look for what else is meant
in the underthought of language.
Words are apparent.

Seen light turns off
to be ambient luminescence,
there and sufficient.
No electricians.

Same sight,
shadows at edge of light,
green field again
where hedgerow finds it.

Read these words then
and see the far trees,
hear the chittering of the birds,
share my ease and dependence.

For Kenneth

It was never a joke.
Hell's not its own reward.
If one even thought of it,
then there it was.

But your classic humor
of the edge, of being about to —
and hanging on even for one last look —
that was truly heroic.

I thought "Sleeping with Women"
sounded like birds settling
in some idyllic edge of meadow
just at night fall.

So there I held on — put my head
down on the pillow,
slept with your words recurring,
fast in their thought.

Hiccups

FOR PHIL

It all goes round,
nothing lost, nothing found —
a common ground.

Outside is in,
that's where it all begins
and where it seems to end.

An ample circle
with center full
of all that's in this world —

or that one—
or still another someone
else had thought was fun.

An echo, a genial emptiness,
a finally common place, a bliss
of this and this and this.

Yesterdays

Sixty-two, sixty-three, I most remember
As time W. C. Williams dies and we are
Back from a hard two years in Guatemala
Where the meager provision of being
Schoolmaster for the kids of the *patrones*
Of two coffee plantations has managed
Neither a life nor money. Leslie dies in
Horror of bank giving way as she and her
Sister and their friends tunnel in to make
A cubby. We live in an old cement brick
Farmhouse already inside the city limits
Of Albuquerque. Or that has all really
Happened and we go to Vancouver where,
Thanks to friends Warren and Ellen Tallman,
I get a job teaching at the University of British
Columbia. It's all a curious dream, a rush
To get out of the country before the sad
Invasion of the Bay of Pigs, that bleak use
Of power. One of my British colleagues
Has converted the assets of himself and
His wife to gold bullion and keeps the
Ingots in a sturdy suitcase pushed under
Their bed. I love the young, at least I
Think I do, in their freshness, their attempt

To find ways into Canada from the western
Reaches. Otherwise the local country seems
Like a faded Edwardian sitcom. A stunned
Stoned woman runs one Saturday night up
And down the floors of the Hydro Electric
Building on Pender with the RCMP in hot
Pursuit where otherwise we stood in long
Patient lines, extending often several blocks
Up the street. We were waiting to get our
Hands stamped and to be given a 12 pack
Of Molson's. I think, I dream, I write the
Final few chapters of *The Island,* the despairs
Gathering at the end. I read Richard Brautigan's
Trout Fishing in America but am too uptight
To enjoy his quiet, bright wit. Then that
Summer there is the great Vancouver Poetry
Festival, Allen comes back from India, Olson
From Gloucester, beloved Robert Duncan
From Stinson Beach. Denise reads "Hypocrite
Women" to the Burnaby ladies and Gary Snyder,
Philip Whalen, and Margaret Avison are there
Too along with a veritable host of the young.
Then it's autumn again. I've quit my job
And we head back to Albuquerque
And I teach again at the university, and
Sometime just about then I must have
Seen myself as others see or saw me,
Even like in a mirror, but could not quite
Accept either their reassuring friendship
Or their equally locating anger. Selfish,
Empty, I kept at it. Thirty-eight years later
I seem to myself still much the same,
Even if I am happier, I think, and older.

Ground Zero

What's after or before
seems a dull locus now
as if there ever could be more

or less of what there is,
a life lived just because
it is a life if nothing more.

The street goes by the door
just like it did before.
Years after I am dead,

there will be someone here instead
perhaps to open it,
look out to see what's there —

even if nothing is,
or ever was,
or somehow all got lost.

Persist, go on, believe.
Dreams may be all we have,
whatever one believe

of worlds wherever they are —
with people waiting there
will know us when we come

when all the strife is over,
all the sad battles lost or won,
all turned to dust.

John's Song

FOR JOHN TAGGART

If ever there is
if ever, if ever
there is, if ever there is.

If ever there is
other than war, other
than where war was, if ever there is.

If ever there is
no war, no more war, no other than us
where war was, where it was.

No more war, dear brother,
no more, no more war
if ever there is.

Emptiness

FOR HELEN

The emptiness up the field where
the barn sits still like an ark, an old
presence I look up there to see, sun
setting, sky gone a vivid streaking of
reds and oranges, a sunset off over the
skirt of woods where my sister's barn sits
up the field with all her determined stuff,
all she brought and put in it, all her
pictures, her pots, her particular books
and icons—so empty, it seems, quickly
emptied of everything there was in it, like
herself the last time in the hospital bed had
been put to face out the big window back of

tv, so one could look out, see down there,
over the field, trees of our place, the house,
woods beyond going off toward Warren, the sight,
she'd say with such emphasis, *I'm where I
want to be!* — could ever Maine be more loved,
more wanted, all our history trailing back
through its desperation, our small people, small
provision, where the poor folk come from like
us, to Massachusetts, to a world where poverty
was a class, like Mrs. Peavey told our mother
she'd never felt poor before, not till she was
given charity by the women of the Women's
Club, her family their annual recipient — empty,
empty, running on *empty,* on nothing, on heart,
on bits and pieces of elegance, on an exquisite frame
of words, on each and every memory she ever had,
on the same will as our mother's, the pinched privacy
of empty purse, the large show of pleasure, of out there
everything, come in, *come in* — she lay there so still,
she had gone into herself, face gone then but for echo
of way she had looked, no longer saw or heard, no more
of any human want, no one wanted. *Go away,*
she might have been saying, *I'm busy today.* Go away.
Hence then to be cremated, to reach the end and be done.

Memory

Somewhere Allen Ginsberg is
recalling his mother's dream
about God, *an old man,* she says,
*living across the river in
Palisades,* obscure, battered,
in a shack with hardly any

provisions. Straight off she asks him,
how could you let the world get
into such a mess, and he can
answer only, *I did the best I could.*
She tells Allen he looks neglected
and there are yellow pee-stains
on his underpants. Hard to hear
God could not do any better
than any of us, just another old
man sitting on some bench or some
chair. I remember it was a urologist
told me how to strip the remaining pee
from my penis by using my finger's
pressure just back of the balls,
the prostate, then bringing it forward
so that the last drops of it would go
into the toilet, not onto my clothes.
Still it's of necessity an imperfect
solution. How stand at a public urinal
seeming to play with oneself? Yet
how not—if that's what it takes not
to walk out, awkward, wide-legged, damp
from the crotch down? I cannot
believe age can be easy for anyone. *On*
Golden Pond may be a pleasant picture
of a lake and that general area of
New Hampshire, but it's not true,
any of it. Please, don't put, if
you can help it, your loved ones in
a care facility, they will only die there.
Everyone's sick there. It's why they've come.
I don't know now what will or
may happen to me. I don't
feel any longer a simple person with

a name. I am like a kid at his,
or her, first day of school. All new,
all surprising. The teacher with
her curious large face, the other
unexpected children, all of us finally
unsure. The seeming fractures of a self
grow ominous, like peaks of old
mountains remembered but faint
in the obscuring fog. Time to push off, do
some push-ups perhaps, take a walk with
the neighbors I haven't spoken to in years.

Generous Life

Do you remember the way we used to sing
in church when we were young
and it was fun to bring your toys with you
and play with them while all the others sung?

My mind goes on its own particular way
and leaves my apparent body on its knees
to get up and walk as far as it can
if it still wants to and as it still proves able.

Sit down, says generous life, *and stay awhile!*
although it's irony that sets the table
and puts the meager food on broken dishes,
pours out the rancid wine and walks away.

On Earth

When I think

When I think of where I've come from
or even try to measure as any kind of
distance those places, all the various
people, and all the ways in which I re-
member them, so that even the skin I
touched or was myself fact of, inside,
could see through like a hole in the wall
or listen to, it must have been, to what
was going on in there, even if I was still
too dumb to know anything—When I think
of the miles and miles of roads, of meals,
of telephone wires even, or even of water
poured out in endless streams down streaks
of black sky or the dirt roads washed clean,
or myriad, salty tears and suddenly it's spring
again, or it was—Even when I think again of
all those I treated so poorly, names, places,
their waiting uselessly for me in the rain and
I never came, was never really there at all,
was moving so confusedly, so fast, so driven
like a car along some empty highway passing,
passing other cars—When I try to think of
things, of what's happened, of what a life is
and was, my life, when I wonder what it meant,
the sad days passing, the continuing, echoing deaths,
all the painful, belligerent news, and the dog still
waiting to be fed, the closeness of you sleeping, voices,
presences, of children, of our own grown children,
the shining, bright sun, the smell of the air just now,
each physical moment, passing, *passing*, it's what
it always is or ever was, just then, just there.

"To think . . ."

To think oneself again
into a tiny hole of self
and pull the covers round
and close the mouth—

shut down the eyes and hands,
keep still the feet,
and think of nothing if one can
not think of it—

a space in whose embrace
such substance is,
a place of emptiness
the heart's regret.

World's mind is after all
an afterthought
of what was there before
and is there still.

Old Song

I'm feeling ok still in some small way.
I've come too far to just go away.
I wish I could stay here some way.

So that what now comes wouldn't only be more
of what's to be lost. What's left would still leave more
to come if one didn't rush to get there.

What's still to say? Your eyes, your hair, your smile,
your body sweet as fresh air, your voice in the clear morning
after another night, *another night,* we lay together, sleeping?

If that has to go, it was never here.
If I know still you're here, then I'm here too
and love you, *and love you.*

For Ric, who Loved this World

The sounds
of his particular

music keep echoing,
stay in the soft

air months after
all's gone to

grass, to lengthening
shadows, to slanting

sun on shifting water,
to the late light's edges

through tall trees —
despite the mind's

still useless,
ponderous thought.

Oh, do you remember . . .

Remember sweet Ed
who despite being dead
embedded
all he said

with lead
could make you dead
too if that's it
for you,

oh dummy
of text,
be it western or mex?
He had grace like a swallow's,

nothing unfallow,
"Elizabethan" at root
with sideburns to boot,
quick on trigger,

also with jigger,
kept an apt time,
walked with a rhyme.
I loved his style

and his guile,
no friend to the loser,
vapid day cruiser,
elsewise bamboozler.

My Ed was quondam god
from human sod
who spoke not loud
but always clear and proud,

often with acid edge—
his pledge
to keep the faith
stays constant to this day.

Paul

I'll never forgive myself for the
violence propelled me at sad Paul
Blackburn, pushed in turn by both
our hopeless wives who were spitting
venom at one another in the heaven
we'd got ourselves to, Mallorca, mid-fifties,
where one could live for peanuts while
writing great works and looking at the
constant blue sea, etc. Why did I fight such
surrogate battles of existence with such
a specific friend as he was for sure?
Our first meeting NYC 1950 we talked two
and a half days straight without leaving the
apartment. He knew Auden and Yeats
by heart and had begun on Pound's lead
translating the Provençal poets, and was
studying with Moses Hadas at NYU. How
sweet this thoughtful beleaguered vulnerable
person whose childhood was full of New
England abusive confusion, his mother the too
often absent poet, Frances Frost! I wish

he were here now, we could go on talking,
I'd have company of my own age in this
drab burned out trashed dump we call the
phenomenal world where he once walked
the wondrous earth and knew its pleasures.

Mediterranean I

This same inexhaustible sea with impenetrable
Same blue look I stepped into when so young I
Had no reason for a life more than to hold on to
The one I had, wife, daughter, and two sons, older,
If seven and five, just, can be measure of more than
A vulnerable innocence. The back wheel of bike,
When brake failed, caught elder son's heel and used
It to stop, stripping the skin off almost to the bone.
I packed the place with ointment and bandaged it, not
Wanting to see how bad it might be, and for days son
Went on hop and hand holds spider fashion until,
Blessedly, it was well again. Oh life, oh miracle of
Day to day existence, sun, food and others! Would
Those who lived with me then believe how much
I loved them? Know how dumbly, persistently, I cared?

Mediterranean II

The cranky low decked freighter with orange stickup
stern cabin we could see from the open window of
this place each day out there on proverbial ocean has
moved away, shifting the focus of that blue to an
implacable distance now going out to a shaded, faded

edge of sky beyond all recalled dreams or places. One
so wanted it to be the old time story of them waiting till
dark at last came and then, with muffled oars, they'd row
into the hidden cove, climb up the adjoining cliff, and
into my waiting heart. How many times so long ago I'd
see the fisherman at nightfall row out into the darkened
sea with their long awkward boats, oars in unison, to what
determined fate, and if there were a world at edge of this
one, there at last they might pull ashore. Now the sea's slur-
ring, recurring sound, its battering, white capped, upon the
rocks, forces both free and unknown to me, have no work
but this tedious recurrence, dreams repeated, insistent, useless.

War

Blur of world is red smear on white page,
metaphors useless, thoughts impotent,
even the sense of days is lost
in the raging militance.

No life other than political,
the fact of family and friends
subjorned to the general
conduct of this bitter abstract.

I look in the mirror
to see old man looking back,
eyes creased, squinting,
finds nothing left.

He longs for significance,
a scratch in the dust, an odor
of some faint fruit, some flower
whose name he'd lost.

Why would they hate him
who fight now insistently
to kill one another
—why not.

Talking

I was trying to think of when rightly
to enter the conversation with all
the others talking thoughtfully,
comfortably. There was no occasion
to say that thirty years in the army was
a long time or that very probably the
world is flatter than one thinks. A star
is as far as one's eye can see? My shirt
had broken buttons I had hid with
my tie. Otherwise I was clean and
reasonably dressed. Yet, impatient to
join in, I could hear my voice landing
suddenly on the edge of another's
comment, me saying I can't now remember
what, just their saying, "What? What?"

Bye and Bye

Faded in face of apparent reality—
As it comes, I see it still goes on and on,
and even now still sitting at this table
is the smiling man who nobody seems to know.

Older, the walls apparently get higher.
No one seemingly gets to look over
to see the people pointing at the sky
where the old planes used to fly over.

I packed my own reality in a bag
and pushed it under the table,
thinking to retrieve it when able
some time bye and bye.

For John Wieners

Glass roses or something else hardly expected—an
Abundance of good will, a kind hand in usual troubles.
Do you hear voices all around you, a sort of whispering,
Echoing silence as if someone had left a window open?

Reading those several times with John, we were first
In a great hall, the Y uptown, where he said he'd heard Auden
Read, and now we did—the great velvet curtains, the useful
Sense of a company in the same place where we now stood, echoing.

Then at Bard, first time I'd met Tom Meyer still a student, and
We, John, Bobbie and me, had driven up from New York together,
In bleak aftermath of Olson's telling John he was going off with Panna,
On the phone in the Chelsea, the blasted heath we were leaving behind.

Sweet, you might say, impeccable gentleman, like Claude Rains, his
Boston accent held each word a particular obligation and value.
I see his face as still a young man, in San Francisco, hearing him
Talking with Joanne, hearing him talk with Joe Dunn, with friends.

When you are a poet as he was, you have no confusions, you write
The words you are given to, you are possessed or protected by a vision.
We are not going anywhere, we are somewhere, here where John is,
Where he's brought us much as he might himself this evening, to listen.

I think of all the impossible loves of my life, all the edges of feeling,
All the helpless reach to others one tried so bitterly to effect, to reach
As one might a hilltop, an edge of sea where the waves can break at last
On the shore. I think of just jumping into darkness, into deep water,

Into nothing one can ever point to as a place out there, just its shadow, a
Beckoning echo of something, a premonition, which does not warn but
    ‹invites.
There is music in pain but not because of it, love in each persistent
    ‹breath.
His was the Light of the World, a lit match or the whole city, burning.

After School

We'd set off into the woods
and would climb trees there
and throw things, shouting
at one another, great shrieking
cries I remember—or would, if
I dreamt—in dreams. *In dreams,*
the poet wrote, *begin responsibilities.*
I thought that was like going to
some wondrous place and all was
waiting there just for you to come
and do what had to be done.

Help!

Help's easy enough
If it comes in time.
Nothing's that hard
If you want to rhyme.

It's when they shoot you
It can hurt,
When the bombs blast off
And you're gone with a squirt.

Sitting in a bunker,
Feeling blue?
Don't be a loser,
It wasn't you—

Wasn't you wanted
To go kill people,
Wasn't you caused
All this trouble.

I can't say, Run!
And I can't say, Hide!
But I still feel
What I feel inside.

It's wrong to kill people
Just to make them pay.
Wrong to blast cities
To make them go away.

You can't take everything
Away from fathers,
Mothers, babies,
Sisters and brothers.

You live in a house?
Wipe your feet!
Take a look around—
Ain't it neat

To come home at night
And have a home,
Be able to sit down
Even all alone?

You think that anyone
Ought to get pushed,
Shoved around
for some old Bush?

Use your head,
Don't get scared,
Stand up straight,
Show what you're made of.

America's heaven,
Let's keep it that way
Which means not killing,
Not running scared,

Not being a creep,
Not wanting to get "them."
Take a chance
And see what they want then.

Maybe just to be safe,
Maybe just to go home,
Maybe just to live
Not scared to the bone,

Not dumped on by world
They won't let you into,
Not forgotten by all
The ones who did it to you.

Sing together!
Make sure it's loud!
One's always one,
But the world's a crowd

Of people, people,
All familiar.
Take a look!
At least it won't kill you.

Shimmer

FOR GRAHAM DEAN

. . . We will all survive, addressed to such glimmering
shimmering transience with its insistent

invitation of other.
So close, so warm, so full.

I
At the edge of the evening then, at
the edge of the river, this edge

of being, as one says, one's own
given body, inexorable *me,* whatever then

can enter, what other stays there, initial,
wave of that changing weather, wind

lifting off sea, cloud fading northward,
even one's own hands' testament, clenched

seeming fists—*pinch me, pinch
ME*... The person inside the mirror

was hiding, came forward only
as you did, was too far inside you, too

much yourself doubling, twinned,
spun in image as you were, a patient

reality to provoke simple witness,
precluded, occluded, still cloudy.

*I am going now
and you can't come with me*...

There is no one here but you.
But who are you, who is it

one takes as life, as so-called reality,
like the mirror's shimmering light

as the sun strikes it, cobwebbed with dust,
layered with its own substance?

Oneself is instance, an echo
mirrored, doubled. Oneself is twin.

II
Looking in, you saw
a faint head there

at some end of what seemed
a mass of things, a layered

density of reflection, which was substance,
someone. Someone looking back.

But no one looked out.
All echo? Semblance?

No self to come home to,
no one to say, *be yourself*—to say, *it's you?*

There is no looking back
or way of being separate.

One can only stand there, *here,* apart
and see another *I* still, wherever, inside oneself.

Sad Walk

I've come to the old echoes again,
know it's where I've been before,
see the same old sun.

But backwards, from all the yesterdays,
it's still the same way,
who gets and who pays.

I was younger then,
walking along still open,
young and having fun.

But now it's just a sad walk
to an empty park,
to sit down and wait, wait to get out.

Caves

So much of my childhood seems
to have been spent in rooms—
at least in memory, the shades

pulled down to make it darker, the
shaft of sunlight at the window's edge.
I could hear the bees then gathering

outside in the lilacs, the birds chirping
as the sun, still high, began to drop.
It was summer, in heaven of small town,

hayfields adjacent, creak and croak
of timbers, of house, of trees, dogs,
elders talking, the lone car turning some

distant corner on Elm Street
way off across the broad lawn.
We dug caves or else found them,

down the field in the woods. We had
shacks we built after battering
at trees, to get branches, made tepee-

like enclosures, leafy, dense and in-
substantial. Memory is the cave
one finally lives in, crawls on

hands and knees to get into.
If Mother says, don't draw
on the book pages, don't color

that small person in the picture, then
you don't unless compulsion, distraction
dictate and you're floating off

on wings of fancy, of persistent seeing
of what's been seen here too, right here,
on this abstracting page. Can I use the green,

when you're done? What's that supposed to be,
says someone. All the kids crowd closer
in what had been an empty room

where one was trying at least
to take a nap, stay quiet, to think
of nothing but oneself.

.

Back into the cave, folks,
and this time we'll get it right?

Or, uncollectively perhaps, it was
a dark and stormy night he

slipped away from the group, got
his mojo working and before

you know it had that there
bison fast on the wall of the outcrop.

I like to think they thought,
though they seemingly didn't, at least

of something, like, where did X put the bones,
what's going to happen next, did she, he or it

really love me? Maybe that's what dogs are for,
but there's no material surviving

pointing to dogs as anyone's best friend, alas.
Still here we are no matter, still hacking away,

slaughtering what we can find to, leaving
far bigger footprints than any old mastodon.

You think it's funny? To have prospect
of being last creature on earth or at best a

company of rats and cockroaches?
You must have a good sense of humor!

Anyhow, have you noticed how everything's
retro these days? Like, something's been here before—

or at least that's the story. *I* think one picture is worth
a thousand words and I *know* one cave fits all sizes.

                .

Much like a fading off airplane's
motor or the sound of the freeway

at a distance, it was all here clearly enough
and no one goes lightly into a cave,

even to hide. But to make such things
on the wall, against such obvious

limits, to work in intermittent dark,
flickering light not even held steadily,

all those insistent difficulties.
They weren't paid to, not that we know of,

and no one seems to have forced them.
There's a company there, tracks

of all kinds of people, old folks
and kids included. Were they having

a picnic? But so far in it's hardly
a casual occasion, flat on back with

the tools of the trade necessarily
close at hand. Try lying in the dark

on the floor of your bedroom and roll
so as you go under the bed and

ask someone to turn off the light.
Then stay there, until someone else comes.

Or paint up under on the mattress the last
thing you remember, dog's snarling visage

as it almost got you, or just what you do
think of as the minutes pass.

                    .

Hauling oneself through invidious
strictures of passage, the height
of the entrance, the long twisting
cramped passage, mind flickers, a lamp
lit flickers, lets image project
what it can, what it will, see there
war as wanting, see life as a river,
see trees as forest, family as
others, see a moment's respite,
hear the hidden bird's song, goes
along, goes along constricted, self-
hating, imploded, drags forward
in imagination of more, has no
time, has hatred, terror, power.
No light at the end of the tunnel.

                    .

The guide speaks of music, the
stalactites, stalagmites making a
possible xylophone, and some
Saturday night-like hoedown
businesses, what, every three
to four thousand years? One
looks and looks and time

is the variable, the determined
as ever river, lost on the way,
drifted on, laps and continues.
The residuum is finally silence,
internal, one's own mind constricted
to focus like any old camera
fixed in its function.

Like all good questions,
this one seems without answer,
leaves the so-called human
behind. It makes its own way
and takes what it's found
as its own and moves on.

.

It's time to go to bed
again, shut the light off,
settle down, straighten
the pillow and try to sleep.
Tomorrow's another day
and that was all thousands
and thousands of years ago,
myriad generations, even
the stones must seem changed.

The gaps in time,
the times one can't account for,
the practice it all took
even to make such images,
the meanings still unclear
though one recognizes
the subject, something has
to be missed, overlooked.

No one simply turns on a light.
Oneself becomes image.
The echo's got in front,
begins again what's over
just at the moment it was done.
No one can catch up, find
some place he's never been to
with friends he never had.

This is where it connects,
not meaning anything one
can know. This is where
one goes in and that's what's to find
beyond any thought or habit,
an arched, dark space, the rock,
and what survives of what's left.

Absence

Sun on the edges of leaves,
patterns of absent pleasure,
all that it meant
now gathered together.

Days all was away
and the clouds were far off
and the sky was heaven itself,
one wanted to stay

alone forever perhaps
where no one was,
and here again it is
still where it was.

The Ball

Room for one and all
around the gathering ball,
to hold the sacred thread,
to hold and wind and pull.

Sit in the common term.
All hands now move as one.
The work continues on.
The task is never done.

Which Way

Which one are you
and who would know.
Which way
would you have come this way.

And what's behind,
beside, before.
If there are more,
why are there more.

On Earth

One's here
and there is still elsewhere
along some road to hell
where all is well –

or heaven
even
where all the saints still wait
and guard the golden gate.

Saying Something

If, as one says, one says
something to another,
does it go on and on then
without apparent end?

Or does it only become talk,
balked by occasion, stopped
because it never got started,
was said to no one?

The Red Flower

What one thinks to hold
Is what one thinks to know,
So comes of simple hope
And leads one on.

The others there the same
With no one then to blame
These flowered circles handed.
So each in turn was bonded.

There the yellow bees will buzz,
And eyes and ears appear
As listening, witnessing hearts
Of each who enters here.

Yet eyes were closed—
As if the inside world one chose
To live in only as one knows.
No thing comes otherwise.

Walk on, on crippled leg,
Because one stumped with cane,
Turned in and upside down
As with all else, bore useless weight.

The way from here is there
And back again, from birth to death,
From egg to echo, flesh to eyeless skull.
One only sleeps to breathe.

The hook, the heart, the body
Deep within its dress, the folds of feelings,
Face to face to face, no bandaged simple place,
No wonder more than this, none less.

The Puzzle

Insoluble.
Neither one nor the other.
A wall.
An undulating water.

A weather.
A point in space.
Waste of time.
Something missed.

The faces.
Trees.
The unicorn
with its horn.

Able
as ready.
Fixed on heart
on head's prerogative.

Which way to go
up down
backward
forward.

In the sky
stars flash by.
Boats
head for heaven.

Down below
the pole
thrusts up
into the diamond.

Found, fills
its echo.
A baby.
Sound.

A Full Cup

Age knows little other than its own complaints.
Times past are not to be recovered ever.
The old man and woman are left to themselves.

When I was young, there seemed little time.
I hurried from day to day as if pursued.
Each thing I discovered, another came to possess me.

Love I could ask no questions of, it was nothing
I ever anticipated, ever thought would be mine.
Even now I wonder if it will escape me.

What I did, I did finally because I had to,
whether from need of my own or that of others.
It is finally impossible to live and work only for pay.

I do not know where I've come from or where I am going.
Life is like a river, a river without beginning or end.
It's been my company all my life, its wetness, its insistent movement.

The only wisdom I have is what someone must have told me,
neither to take nor to give more than can be simply managed.
A full cup carried from the well.

Old Story

FROM *THE DIARY OF FRANCIS KILVERT*

One bell wouldn't ring loud enough.
So they beat the bell to hell, Max,
with an axe, show it who's boss,
boss. Me, I dreamt I dwelt in
some place one could relax
but I was wrong, wrong, *wrong.*
You got a song, man, sing it.
You got a bell, man, ring it.

Later (Wrightsville Beach)

Crusoe again, confounded, confounding purposes,
cruising, looking around for edges of the familiar,
the places he was in back then,

wherever, all the old sand and water.
How much he thought to be there he can't remember.
Shipwreck wasn't thinkable at least until

after it happened, and then he began at the edge,
the beach, going forward, backward, until he found place again.
Even years slipped past in the background.

The water, waves, sand, backdrop of the houses,
all changed now by the locals, the tourists,
whoever got there first and what they could make of it.

But his story is real too, the footprint, the displacement
when for the first time another is there, not just imagined,
and won't necessarily agree with anything, won't go away.

Dover Beach (Again)

The waves keep at it,
Arnold's Aegean Sophocles heard,
the swell and ebb,
the cresting and the falling under,

each one particular and the same —
Each day a reminder, each sun in its world, each face,
each word something one hears
or someone once heard.

Echo

Walking, the way it used to be,
talking, thinking — being in,
on the way — days after anything
went or came, with no one,
someone, having or not having a way.
What's a life if you look at it,
what's a hat if it doesn't fit.

Wish

I am
transformed into a clam.

I will
be very, very still.

So natural be,
and never 'me'

alone so far from home
a stone

would end it all
but for this tall

enduring tree,
the sea,

the sky
and I.

Here

Up a hill and down again.
Around and in—

Out was what it was all about
but now it's done.

At the end was the beginning,
just like it said or someone did.

Keep looking, keep looking,
keep looking.

TO MY / LITTLE:
PEN'S
VALENTINE

To My   *Dear* (begin again)
Little   *Yo*(u)
               W(ere my)
Dear   *Fr*(iend)
Yo
Wh   *To My*
Fr   *Little* To
               My
Do *better*   Love
To
Wh*ere*
Fr*om*

Valentine for You

Wherefrom, whereto
the thought to do—

Wherewith, whereby
the means themselves now lie—

Wherefor, wherein
such hopes of reconciling heaven—

Even the way is changed
without you, even the day.

Unpublished Poems

Poets

Friend I had in college told
me he had seen as kid out the
window in backyard of an
apartment in upscale Phila-
delphia the elder Yeats walking
and wondered if perhaps he
was composing a poem or else
in some way significantly thinking.
So later he described it, then
living in a pleasant yellowish
house off Harvard Square,
having rooms there, where,
visiting I recall quick sight of
John Berryman who had been
his teacher and was just leaving
as I'd come in, on a landing of
the stairs I'd just come up, the
only time and place I ever did.

Jumping with Jackson

Can't say much
Of age and such,

Just it's fun to breathe
And take one's ease

With a friend like you
Who keeps it true

To life and what
We came here for and got.

Harvey's Hip

Beauty's in eye of the proverbial beholder,
but when you're older,
you get bolder.

Harvey says, "Hold still, bro, so I can get you,
let me look hard at you, stare at you, see what you
never thought I'd know how to."

It all fits in his impeccable scheme
like dreams find room for one and all, it seems,
and "inside out" is what it always comes to mean.

Harvey knows—from the hair on your head
to the bottoms of your shoes, to what you do in bed—
even who you were talking to and what they said.

Alice

Happiness is its own reward,
not bought or sold,
not earned or even thought of.

Pleasure's its echo,
sudden burst of sun,
the weather changing everything

when mind can't follow
after all it was fact of,
what's then left of feeling.

Your name *Alice* says that you are *noble,*
hold *true*—but wonder for me is all you are and do,
all of you

Credits

The following texts included in this volume were originally published as follows:

"Preface: Old Poetry." In *So There: Poems 1976–1983*. New York: New Directions, 1998. Copyright © Robert Creeley. Reprinted by permission of New Directions Publishing Corp.

Hello: A Journal, February 29–May 3, 1976. New York: New Directions, 1978. Reprinted in *So There*.

Later. New York: New Directions, 1979. Reprinted in *So There*.

Mirrors. New York: New Directions, 1983. Reprinted in *So There*.

Memory Gardens. New York: New Directions, 1986. Reprinted in *Just in Time: Poems 1984–1994*. (New York: New Directions, 2001).

Windows. New York: New Directions, 1990. Reprinted in *Just in Time*.

Echoes. New York: New Directions, 1994. Reprinted in *Just in Time*.

Life & Death. New York: New Directions, 1998.

If I were writing this. New York: New Directions, 2003.

On Earth. Berkeley and Los Angeles: University of California Press, 2006.

Epigraphs appear here by permission as follows:

Alighieri, Dante. *Purgatorio*. Trans. Laurence Binyon. London: MacMillan and Co., 1938. By permission of The Society of Authors, on behalf of the Laurence Binyon Estate.

Ginsberg, Allen. "Kaddish." In *Collected Poems, 1947–1980*. New York: HarperCollins, 1984. Reprinted by permission of HarperCollins and the Wylie Agency.

——. "Memory Gardens." In *Collected Poems, 1947–1980*. New York: HarperCollins, 1984. Reprinted by permission of HarperCollins and the Wylie Agency.

Kavanagh, Patrick. "Prelude." In *Collected Poems*. New York: W.W. Norton, 1973. Reprinted by permission of the Estate of Patrick Kavanagh, Devin-Adair Publishers, Old Greenwich, CT. Copyright holder. ALL RIGHTS RESERVED.

Lowry, Malcolm. *Dark as the Grave wherein My Friend Is Laid*. London: Jonathan Cape, 1968. Reprinted by permission of The Random House Group Ltd.

Olson, Charles. "When do poppies bloom . . ." In *The Maximus Poems*, ed. by George F. Butterick. Berkeley: University of California Press, 1985. Reprinted by permission of University of California Press and the Estate of Charles Olson.

St. Vincent Millay, Edna. "Renascence." In *Collected Poems of Edna St. Vincent Millay*. New York: Harper Perennial, 1981. Reprinted by permission of the Edna St. Vincent Millay Society. Copyright 1912, 1940 by Edna St. Vincent Millay.

Stevens, Wallace. "Anecdote of the Jar." In *The Collected Poems of Wallace Stevens*. New York: Vintage, 1990. Reprinted by permission of Alfred A. Knopf, Inc.

Ziarek, Krzysztof. From *Inflected Language: Toward a Hermeneutics of Nearness: Heidegger, Levinas, Stevens, Celan*. Albany: State University of New York Press, 1994. Reprinted by permission of SUNY Press.

Zukofsky, Louis. Original publication unknown. All Louis Zukofsky material Copyright Paul Zukofsky; the material may not reproduced, quoted, or used in any manner whatsoever without the explicit and specific permission of the copyright holder.

Index of Titles and First Lines

Titles appear in roman type. First lines appear in italics.

DESIGNER
J.G. Braun

TEXT
9.5/12.5 Rotis Serif

DISPLAY
Rotis Serif

COMPOSITOR
BookMatters, Berkeley

PRINTER + BINDER
Thomson-Shore, Inc.